I met a farmer who's a magician. How do you know? He told me he was going to turn his cow into a field.

What do you call neurotic octopus? A crazy mixed-up squid.

Have a bumper fun time

Where do tadpoles go when they lose their tails? To a retail shop.

Published by Holland Enterprises Limited,
18 Bourne Court, Southend Road, Woodford Green, Essex U.K.
Copyright © World International Publishing Ltd.,

Item Reference No.773H   ISBN 1 85038 288 3

WORD GAMES

YOU CAN PLAY WORD GAMES INDOORS WHEN IT'S TOO COLD OR WET TO GO OUTSIDE, OR IN THE GARDEN WHEN IT'S TOO HOT TO DO ANYTHING ELSE.

The Minister's Cat

The first player thinks of an adjective beginning with 'A' and says, 'The Minister's cat is an <u>A</u>wful cat.' The next player thinks of an adjective beginning with 'B' and says, 'The Minister's cat is an <u>A</u>wful, <u>B</u>old cat,' and so on, each player calling out all the adjectives that have been used before, and then adding a new one in alphabetical order.

Anyone who makes a mistake or takes too long drops out until there is only one player— the winner— left.

ROUND the WORLD

PLAYER ① CALLS OUT ANY PLACE NAME THAT COMES TO MIND, SAY 'ABERDEEN'. THE NEXT TO GO HAS TO CALL OUT ANOTHER PLACE NAME STARTING WITH THE LAST LETTER OF THE FIRST NAME, e.g. 'NEWCASTLE', AND SO ON.

A TYPICAL GAME COULD GO: ABERDEEN, NEWCASTLE, EDINBURGH, HULL, LONDON, NOTTINGHAM, MANCHESTER...

SID'S FAVOURITE WORD GAME

Every night before he goes to bed, Sid thinks of a word. If he can remember it when he wakes up next morning, he stays in bed for another ten minutes. If he can't, he stays in bed until he can!

4

WHOSE HAT?

Here you see six different people—A to F—and underneath them there are six hats—1 to 6—of various types. Can you find out which of the hats belongs to which person in their correct order?

1

King James I (1566-1625) sold Canada to Sir William Alexander for one Scottish penny in 1621.

Intense cold was to blame for Big Ben striking only once at midnight on 28 January 1947.

Prince Philip is the holder of UK passport No 1, the Queen not requiring one.

GIVE US A CLUE!

INSPECTOR CLUELESS IS AFTER A TOUGH CRIMINAL—
CAN YOU HELP THE INSPECTOR FIND HIM?

① HE DOESN'T WEAR GLASSES ✓
② HE ISN'T CLEAN SHAVEN ✓
③ HE DOESN'T HAVE A HAT ✓
④ HE'S SMILING ✓
⑤ HE HAS A BOW-TIE ✓
⑥ HE ISN'T BALD ✓
⑦ HE HAS A SCAR ✓
⑧ HE HAS BIG EARS ✓

BEE MAZE

In which of the tunnels will the bee find himself?

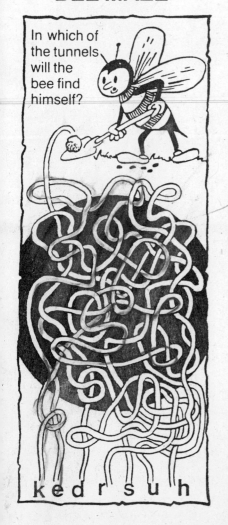

k e d r s u h

Limerick Fun

A racing driver called Neil
Went crazy behind the car wheel.
He drove his new Rover
From Brands Hatch to Dover,
And into the sea just past Deal.

An old lady who came from Kilbride,
Ate so many apples she died!
The apples fermented
Inside the lamented,
Making cider inside 'er inside!

A girl from Cardiff called Gwen
Stood at the foot of Big Ben.
At one o'clock
The clang was a shock;
Said she, 'I'm glad it's not ten!'

A policeman when out on the beat,
Helped a lady to cross the street.
As he lifted his arm
He said, 'You'll come to no harm,'
Then a lorry ran over his feet.

A very fat man from Boston
Went to a river and crossed on
A bridge that was weak,
Which spanned a creek;
And that was the trip he was lost on!

There once was a brown and white duck
Who one day was down on his luck.
When a hunter's gun fired
That poor duck expired,
For that dumb bird forgot he should duck.

A gentleman dining in Kew
Once found a dead mouse in his stew:
'Don't wave it about,'
Said the head-waiter, Stout,
'Or the others will ask for one too!'

Foggy

* Begin

End *

Take the plane safely through the fog

8

The Domesday Book, a survey of England completed in 1086, actually consists of two large volumes, now kept at the Public Records Office in London.

The common shrew is the shortest-lived mammal. It lives for only about two years.

In the language of the Mississippi river-boat pilots, 'Mark Twain' meant a depth of 2 fathoms, indicating safe water.

Let's draw a
CHIMPANZEE

Chimpanzees are very clever animals. They can be taught to do many things that most other animals cannot do, riding bikes and eating and drinking at a table like humans. We see them mainly at zoos and circuses, but their natural home is in Africa. Chimpanzees can stand and walk upright, but they usually move around on both their hands and feet. They live in small family groups, mostly eating fruit and vegetables and maybe birds' eggs and insects. Chimpanzees spend most of their time in trees, even building themselves a kind of bed to sleep in!

1

Let's draw a
POLAR BEAR

2

The polar bear lives in the Arctic, which is as far North as you can go. It lives on the ice packs which form on the sea when the weather gets very cold. Polar bears eat fish, seals and dead animals. They never feel the cold, even in the sea, because they have very thick fur on their bodies. They are also good swimmers and will swim around in the icy sea for hours until they find some food. When the young are about to be born, the mother makes a deep hole in the ice and covers the entrance with snow so that she can keep her young warm.

"And the children are quite fond of him really"

Do you believe in ghosts? I never did, but now...

"But you couldn't have seen him; he's just . . . well, he's just not around any more."

"But it was him," argued Robert, his blue eyes flashing through his lopsided glasses. He never put them on properly and he was always chewing the ends. "You ask Stephen and Swat. They were with me." And he made a sly grab for his fifth piece of bread and butter under cover of the conversation.

by Terry Stevens

Jenny, the other member of staff on duty with me, said nothing, but looked straight at me with her big brown eyes. The other eight children said nothing, but were waiting to hear my answer to Robert's retort. Davin, a boy with a similar handicap to Robert, saved me the trouble.

"Oh well, I thought he was supposed to be in Switzerland?"

He was, and I said as much.

"You must have seen a ghost then," sniggered ten-year-old Laureen, who was afraid of anything even slightly sinister or scary. She fidgeted in her wheelchair and looked at me.

We were in the living-room having tea when this conversation had arisen, one dark and damp November evening. Robert, Stephen and Allen Swatilski had supposedly seen Tony out on the playground, not ten minutes ago, when returning from a school Christmas concert practice. The school buildings were on the other side of the playground from the big old house which was home to the fifty-odd children at Valley Hill School. Tony had been a member of staff here for two years, until his departure six months ago for another appointment in Switzerland. He was on his way there when he was taken ill, and he died within a couple of days. The children hadn't been told of this, and so it was highly unlikely that they were making up this story of seeing him out of morbidness.

Tea continued, and finished with a different subject. It seemed to be a case of mistaken identity in the half-light. After all, only last week three of them had mistaken somebody else in the village for me, and that was in broad daylight. Allen hadn't even seen Tony before, as Allen was a new arrival at the beginning of term.

So that was that. Or, at least, that's what I thought, until nearly a week later. I was in the school building that particular evening, setting up the table tennis in readiness for the following evening's club for over-twelves, when Mrs Harris, the school cleaner, came into the hall.

"Oh, it's you," she said. She put emphasis on the word 'you' as if she was expecting someone else.

"Yes, it's me," I replied, continuing with my task.

"Well, I looked out of the window a little while ago and I

13

What do you get if you cross a skunk with a boomerang?
A smell you can't get rid of.

Doctor, doctor, I think I'm a pigeon.
I'll tweet you in a moment.

How does a ghost pass through a locked door?
It uses a skeleton key.

Are vampires mad?
Well, they're often bats.

Football master: Alec, why didn't you stop that ball?
Alec: Because I thought that's what the net was for, Sir.

Knock, knock.
Who's there?
Saul.
Saul who?
Saul over and done with.

thought I saw Tony out on the playground, but it must have been you."

A distinctly eerie feeling affected the nape of my neck on hearing Tony's name mentioned again. It felt as if the hairs on the back of my head were standing to attention.

"Tony?" was all I could think of saying.

"Yes. I thought for a moment he was paying us a visit. I thought it was a bit soon for that, after all he's only been gone a few months. Well, I must get on. Will you lock up the hall when you've done?"

I replied that I would and she said goodnight.

I immediately thought of three things. Firstly, I had only been in the building a few minutes at the very most; secondly, I had not crossed the playground, but had entered from the side; and thirdly, Mrs Harris didn't know that Tony was dead. I might add that, fourthly, I suddenly felt quite scared, even though Tony had been my friend.

That was on Friday.

The weekend came and went without further incident concerning Tony.

Then, at tea on Monday, Robert was very quiet. That was unusual for Robert, and when he was quiet there was usually a reason for it.

I didn't remark on it as I knew that if something was worrying him I would soon know. I was proved to be correct as Robert asked to see me in the boys' bedroom after tea was cleared away. Allen was also in there. The latter looked at Robert, who was sitting on his bed looking at the floor between his legs. He didn't look up at me when he started talking.

"You know last week I told you that I thought we had seen Tony?"

"Yes?"

"Well, we saw him again today," he said quickly, looking at me for the first time.

"Where?"

"We were coming out of school again, after our practice. Didn't we, Allen?"

Allen confirmed this.

"What was he like?" I asked Allen, knowing he hadn't seen him before.

Allen gave me his description. It fitted perfectly, even down to the old black corduroy jacket that he very often wore for work.

"And this time Veronica and Anne were with us too," added Robert.

"Veronica saw him first actually," said Allen.

I asked where and Robert answered. "He was standing by the big tree next to the woodwork room," he said.

The woodwork room adjoined the school buildings at a right angle.

"What was he doing?"

Robert looked at the floor again before answering. "Just standing there, sort of . . . and well, just standing . . ."

"And smiling," added Allen.

Evidently Robert didn't want to say it. But now he looked up again and confirmed this. "Yes, smiling at us. Veronica called out to him, but then he was gone."

"Gone?"

15

"Yes. We came out of the school, you see; Veronica saw him and called to him, and then we all stood and watched. But when we started to go over to him, he waved to us and then seemed to disappear behind the big tree in the corner."

There was silence. Robert and Allen looked at me as if they were *willing* me to believe their story. In fact, it wasn't that I disbelieved what they had said, it was just that I didn't know whether or not I believed in ghosts, or even whether or not I *should* believe in ghosts, because it certainly seemed to me that they had actually seen Tony.

"I thought he was abroad?" asked Robert.

"Well, he did in fact set off . . ." I began. But then what should I say? I didn't want to scare the living daylights out of them, but on the other hand death is something that they were bound to encounter in some form or another through their lives.

Fortunately, I was saved by Jenny, who barged in to announce that Robert's mother was on the telephone and that Jo, Allen's housemother, wanted him. I told them to be careful who was around when they mentioned this business, thinking of the younger ones, and that we'd see what came of it all.

Later that evening I was helping Davin get out of the bath when he asked, "Do you think they've been seeing a ghost?"

Obviously Robert and Allen had been sharing their experiences with Davin.

"I don't know, Davin, really I don't." That was quite true, I didn't, and if I thought otherwise I would have said so earlier. All I knew was that they weren't making up the story. I know Robert well enough to tell that much.

"It does seem funny though, doesn't it?" he continued.

"Yes. It certainly does."

"Oh well, I wish I could see him. He doesn't seem to be a scary type of ghost. If he *is* a ghost, of course," he added as an afterthought.

That was true. He didn't seem a scary type of ghost at all. In fact I suppose there was no reason why he *should* scare the children. After all, he loved them enough when he was here. Heavens, I was even beginning to believe there was a ghost after all.

Then Davin asked the question I had hoped would never come, although he did avoid using the operative word.

"Is Tony still alive then?"

"No, he isn't. He died of an illness shortly after he left here." Robert had come into the bathroom and heard this.

"I thought so," said Robert, "because he couldn't be alive if he was a ghost."

Children never cease to amaze adults. Sometimes they accept things easier than one imagines they would. In this case they had obviously thought of the possibility of him being dead before; probably the first time they had thought that they had seen him.

Then came a spate of questions like why he'd come back and what was a ghost exactly, to all of which I could only answer vaguely, if at all. I suppose I was relieved to find that they weren't frightened at all. They took it just like a couple of normal twelve-year-olds probably would, as an adventure of a sort.

Davin scooted out of the bathroom and when I asked what the hurry was, he said that he was going downstairs to see if he could see Tony from the bedroom window. I think that's more than I would have done.

During the following week, Tony appeared several more times in the dark evenings, and each time to more of the children. Never when there was a member of staff around. And he was always smiling at them.

He didn't even appear as a ghost is supposed to appear. I mean there was never anything 'ghostly' in his appearance. He looked just like a normal person, except that he was slightly transparent and, of course, he couldn't speak or be heard.

He never frightened the children, and in turn the children were never frightened of him. Even Laureen, when she first saw him, only paled slightly, and Robert said she even

Teacher: Why don't you write more clearly?
Alec: Then you'll realise I can't spell!

What do you get if you cross a Tyrannosaurus with a cow?
A monster that eats anyone that tries to milk it.

waved back at him, which evidently made Tony smile even more. Then he vanished behind his favourite tree.

Jenny and I were the first members of staff to see him, and he was just as the children had described. Only one thing was different. It was broad daylight. The children — and I'm sure they had all seen him by now — were outside playing during afternoon break.

The two of us had come over to discuss some point regarding the coming concert with Mrs Jones, the teacher in charge of the production, when I happened to catch sight of him, standing with a bemused look on his face, near to a group of children playing catch. Some of the children had already seen him and were waving to him. Others just continued to play.

It was an incredible sight. Not one of the children was afraid of him. The three of us surveyed the scene from inside the school and all we could manage to say between the three of us, came in the form of, "Well I never," from Mrs Jones.

Then Tony saw us . . . and waved. I waved back, feeling slightly silly. Then he turned and 'walked' slowly back to his tree.

> *Man in a restaurant: Have you got asparagus? Waiter: NO, we don't serve sparrows and my name's not Gus.*
>
> *Doctor, doctor, those pills you gave me to make me stronger aren't doing any good at all.*
> *How can you tell?*
> *I can't unscrew the bottle.*

> *Knock, knock.*
> *Who's there?*
> *Joy.*
> *Joy who?*
> *J'oil your bike regularly?*
>
> *Why do idiots eat biscuits?*
> *Because they're crackers.*
>
> *What is written at the top of an idiot's ladder?*
> *Stop.*

This was all a year ago. Tony is still there, still wandering around the playground, just smiling at, waving at and watching the children, as if he is their protector. Perhaps he is. I like to think that he is there because he was at his happiest with the children; but I don't really know, neither do I understand. All I know is that we all just accept him, and like having him around, I suppose.

Funnily enough, no one outside the school can see him.

I didn't realize this until one day soon after I had first seen him when I was showing a group of students around. We had reached the school just in time to see the children come out for their morning break, and I was introducing Mr Harris the teacher on playground duty to them, when I noticed Tony looking at me a few feet away.

I thought I should introduce him, as perhaps they wouldn't realize he was slightly transparent, and so I pointed to where he was standing and said, "And this is Tony who used . . . er . . . who is . . ."

Well, what was I supposed to say? In any case they

didn't see him, and some even looked straight through him. It was then that I realized, and so did Mr Harris, giving me a knowing look.

Tony was laughing, showing all his teeth, and so were some of the more observant children.

Yes, he is still here, on and off, and usually when the children are around, although he never ventures from the playground. We have had new staff and children since his first appearance, and telling the children about it is not so much a problem as telling the staff. Imagine what you say to them when they ask who the strange character is out on the playground.

"Oh, him. Well, that's Tony. He used to work here."

"Used to work here? What does he do now then?"

"Ah, well, he's a ghost now, you see."

"A ghost!"

"Yes. But don't worry. He's very friendly, and the children are quite fond of him really."

And if you believe that
you'll believe anything!

GARDENING WITH DAFFY DILL

HOLD A SUNFLOWER GROWING COMPETITION.

BUY A PACKET OF SUNFLOWER SEEDS.

PLANT THE SEEDS IN A SUNNY, SHELTERED SPOT, AND WATER THEM. TIE A PLANT LABEL WITH YOUR NAME ON IT ONTO A STICK AND PUSH IT INTO THE GROUND BY THE SIDE OF YOUR SEED.

DAFFY   SID

WHICH OF YOU HAS GROWN THE BIGGEST FLOWER?

SMIRK

1st

Did you know that some sunflowers have reached well over 6m (20ft) high?!

21

 **Sparkling** Find your way to the diamond.

23

WRITING

BALLPOINT

COPY

DATE
DEMY

FOOLSCAP
FOUNTAIN (pen)

NOTE

PADS
PAPYRUS
PARCHMENT
PENCIL
PENS

REED

STYLUS

TABLET
TYPING

VELLUM

T	Q	P	N	M	Y	P	O	C	B
U	N	O	A	Y	U	S	E	A	I
S	T	E	M	C	T	L	L	N	F
E	U	E	M	Y	S	L	L	O	S
T	D	R	L	H	P	L	U	E	L
Y	A	U	Y	O	C	N	O	I	V
P	S	B	I	P	T	R	C	O	R
I	A	N	L	A	A	N	A	E	F
N	T	D	I	E	E	P	E	P	L
G	L	N	S	P	T	D	A	T	E

Clue: Old type of pen (5 letters)

3

Europe's three active volcanoes are Vesuvius, near Naples, Etna in Sicily, and Stromboli on Lapari Island. All are technically Italian.

A runcible spoon, immortalized by Edward Lear, is a kind of fork with three broad prongs, used for pickles.

Only three kinds of snake are found in Great Britain: the venomous viper or adder; the harmless grass snake; and the rare smooth snake of southern England.

24

SECRET CODE

3rd. letter	4th. letter	5th. letter	6th. letter	8th. letter	1st. letter

Work out what the pictures represent and then place the appropriate letters into the blank spaces below to reveal an American city.

They all go in

FIT THE PICTURE NAMES INTO THE CIRCLE.

25

An American farmer has grown a whole field of four-leaved clover and now has a worldwide trade.

A tortoise takes four hours to travel 1 mile (1.5 km).

CAR GAMES

① LIMB-O

THIS IS A GOOD GAME TO PLAY WHEN YOU'RE DRIVING THROUGH TOWNS. EACH TIME YOU PASS A PUB, LOOK AT THE NAME. THE PERSON WHOSE TURN IT IS GAINS A POINT FOR EVERY LEG, AND LOSES ONE FOR EACH ARM SUGGESTED BY THE SIGN. FOR EXAMPLE, IF YOU PASS 'THE DOG AND FOX' YOU GET EIGHT POINTS (EIGHT LEGS); 'THE GEORGE AND DRAGON' EARNS SIX POINTS (TWO FOR GEORGE, FOUR FOR THE DRAGON). PASS 'THE QUEEN'S ARMS' AND YOU LOSE A POINT FOR EACH ARM. PLAYERS' TURNS LAST UNTIL THEY PASS A PUB THAT DOESN'T PRODUCE A SCORE e.g. 'THE BELL', 'THE CONSTITUTION', OR ANYTHING ELSE WITHOUT LEGS OR ARMS.

What about 'The Caterpillar and Centipede'?

② the TRAFFIC JAM GAME

NEXT TIME YOU'RE STUCK IN A BORING TRAFFIC SNARL-UP, GET EVERYONE IN THE CAR TO LOOK AROUND UNTIL YOU START MOVING. WHOEVER GOES FIRST ASKS THE OTHER PASSENGERS A QUESTION SUCH AS 'WHAT WAS THE COLOUR OF THE CAR ALONGSIDE?' OR 'WAS THE MAN IN THE CAR BEHIND WEARING A TIE?' HE CARRIES ON ASKING THE QUESTIONS UNTIL SOMEONE GIVES A RIGHT ANSWER, SCORING A POINT EACH TIME HE STUMPS THE PASSENGERS. WHOEVER ANSWERS CORRECTLY TAKES OVER AS QUESTIONER.

What cars like traffic jams?

Datsun Cherries!

Why does a witch ride on a broom?
    Because a vacuum cleaner is too heavy to fly.

NOT IF YOU PUT JET-ENGINES ON IT!

Teacher: 'Did your father help you with you[r] homework?'
Alec: 'No, I got it wrong all by myself!'

If cows could fly, what might you get?
    A pat on the head.

Mum: How did you get on at school today, Alec?
Alec: OK apart from pottery. The teacher didn't like what I made.
Mum: What was that?
Alec: A dreadful mess.

Knock, knock.
Who's there?
Lever.
Lever who?
Leave a drop for me.

Girlfriend: 'Do you realize it takes three sheep just to make one sweater?'
Alec: 'Really? I didn't even know that sheep could knit!'

What do you get if you cross a parrot with a centipede?
    A walkie talkie.

Did you hear about the cross-eyed teacher who had no control over her pupils?

The maths teacher was teaching his class decimals. He wrote 12.30 on the board and said he was going to multiply by ten, rubbing the decimal point out.
    'Where's the point now, Alec?'
    'On the duster, Sir.'

Teacher: What's the longest word in the dictionary, Alec?
Alec: Elastic! Because it stretches as far as you want it to.

'Please Miss,' said Alec. 'I've got a cousin with three feet.'
    'Good gracious! How odd! How do you know?'
    'Mum got a letter from her sister this morning and it said that her eldest boy had grown another foot during the last year.'

Doctor, doctor, I keep thinking I'm a pair of curtains!
    Pull yourself together, man!

Why did Smart Alec's eccentric Uncle Cuthbert hide under the bed?
    Because he thought he was a little potty.

Geography teacher: Alec, where would you see a fjord?
Alec: In a Norwegian garage Sir?

Did you hear about the schoolboy who was ticked off because of his careless appearance?
    He hadn't appeared in school for half a term.

'Your daughter's only five and she can spell her name backwards? Why that is remarkable.' The headmistress was talking to a parent who was trying to impress her with the child's academic prowess so that she would be accepted into the school.
    'Yes, we're very proud of her,' said the mother.
    'And what is your daughter's name?'
    'Anna.'

Pupil: I keep seeing little black dots before my eyes.
Teacher: Have you seen the doctor?
Pupil: No Miss! Just little black dots.

Father: 'Why don't you play cards with Billy any more?'
Alec: 'Would you play cards with someone who cheats?'
Father: 'No.'
Alec: 'Neither will Billy.'

Alec: 'My cousin died of lead poisoning.'
Friend: 'How did that happen?'
Alec: 'Someone shot him!'

Natural history teacher: Alec! What's a slug?
Alec: A snail with a housing problem.

Mum: 'Here's three bags of Christmas sweets for you and your sister.'
Alec: 'It's difficult to divide three, so I'll keep one and divide the other two!'

How do you stop a pig from smelling?
Put a clothes-peg over its nose.

Tony: 'My mum says that cleanliness is next to godliness.'
Alec: 'With my little sister it's next to impossible.'

'Thomas Edison once said that genius is 1% inspiration and 99% perspiration.'
'I hate to think of anyone that sweaty handling electricity!'

Alec: 'This restaurant must have a very clean kitchen.'
Waiter: 'Thank you. Why do you say that?'
Alec: 'Everything tastes of soap.'

'I didn't come here to be insulted.'
'Where do you usually go?'

Teacher: Alec! If you had a five pound note and you asked your granny for another one, what would you have?
Alec: Five pounds.
Teacher: You don't know your arithmetic.
Alec: And you don't know my granny.

'When Johnny goes to a zoo he needs two tickets.'
'Why?'
'One to get in and one to get out.'

Biology teacher: What's the difference between a female skeleton and a male skeleton?
Alec: The female's the one with the jaw open.

What smells of fish and travels at twice the speed of sound?
A Concorde pilot's tuna sandwich.

BUT I HATE TUNA SANDWICHES!

'Alec,' said the teacher one day. 'If it takes fifteen men twelve hours to build a wall, how long will it take five men?'
'No time at all, Sir,' said Alec. 'The fifteen have already built it.'

How many wallies does it take to peel an onion?
Two. One to hold the knife and one to turn the onion.

'Waiter, what's this fly doing in my soup?'
'It looks like the backstroke!'

Sports master: What are the best vegetables for athletes?
Alec: Runner beans.

29

Pentominoes are shapes made from five attached squares (dominoes require only two). Twelve different combinations are possible, and they can all be fitted together to form a rectangle.

Brass instruments such as the cornet, trumpet, trombone and French horn can play five basic notes, though their range is increased by the use of such devices as valves and slides.

There are five precious metals: platinum, gold, silver, palladium and iradium.

CROSSWORD

Across

1. Businessman's luggage (9)
6. Fire grid (5)
9. Child's bed (3)
10. Sound in mind (4)
11. Girl's name (3)
16. Monster (4)
19. Anger (3)
20. Hard wood (5)
21. Schemers (9)

Down

1. Entreats (4)
2. Persia (4)
3. Enemy (3)
4. Chief (4)
5. Consumes (4)
7. Knock (3)
8. Beverage (3)
12. Superior person (3)
13. Container for 8 Down (3)
14. Tie (4)
15. Wagers (4)
17. Triangular piece of land (4)
18. Organs (4)
20. Urge (3)

There have been six Great Fires of London: in 798, 982, 1212, 1666, 1800 and 1940. That of September, 1666 lasted over four days and destroyed 13,200 houses and numerous churches and public buildings. Remarkably, the death toll was only six.

All snowflakes, though markedly different in appearance, are constructed on a hexagon.

A light year is equal to about 6 million million miles (9.6 million million m).

NOISES

BOOM
BRAY

CHIRP
CLANG
CURR

DING
DRONE

FIZZ

GRUNT

HISS
HONK

HOOT
HUMS

JINGLE

MEOW

NOISE

PEEP
PING
PURR

RASP
ROAR
RUMBLE

SIZZLE

THUD

WHINE

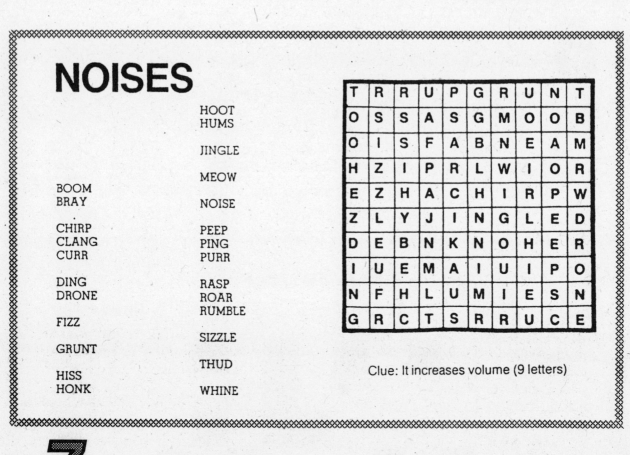

Clue: It increases volume (9 letters)

Light travels the equivalent distance to seven times round the world in just one second.

The seven deadly sins are: pride, avarice, lust, anger, gluttony, envy and sloth.

The Romans used seven symbols for numerals: I, V, X, L, C, D, M.

The numbers on a die (singular of dice) are so arranged that those on opposite faces always add up to seven.

Snakes and ladders

Find a way between the stars.

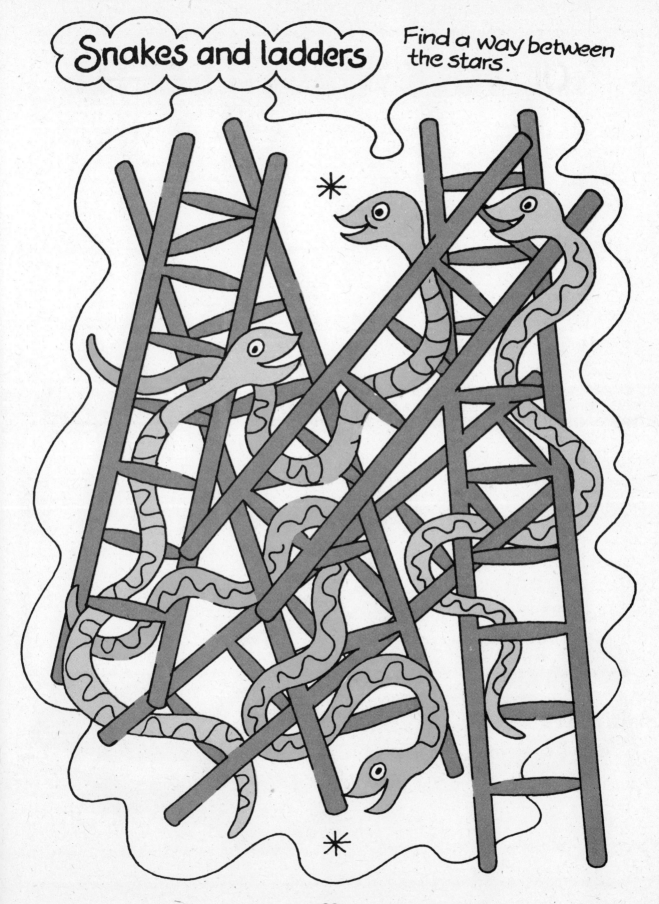

33

Let's draw a
VOLKSWAGEN BEETLE

The Volkswagen Beetle was designed by Ferdinand Porsche. It was specially built for ordinary people at a price that ordinary people could afford. The German people were to pay £50 for the car when it first appeared in 1938.

The Second World War stopped the car from selling in enormous numbers, but after the war the car became more popular. The thousandth car was produced in March 1946 and the millionth in July 1953. By 1977 more than 19 million cars had been made. The Beetle is still a fairly cheap car and the design has hardly changed in forty years.

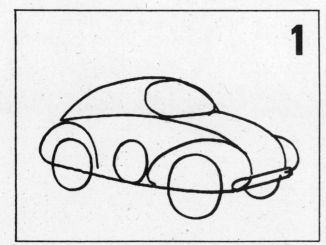

1

2

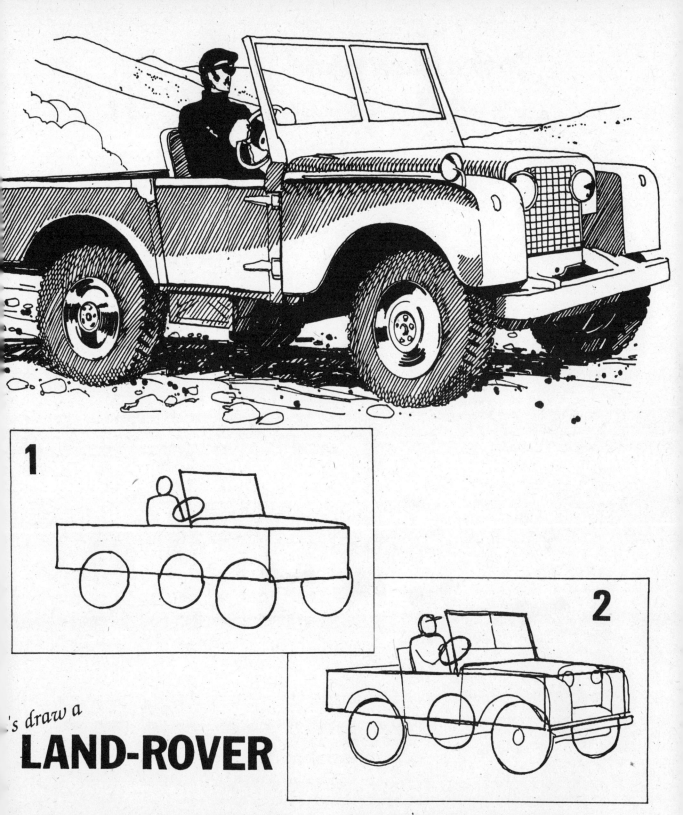

1

2

LAND-ROVER

One famous car-making firm is Rover. Rover have been making cars for a very long time and are now part of a large car-making firm called British Leyland. One rather special, and different, car that they have made is the Land-Rover.

The Land-Rover is a different shape from most cars. It is much squarer and larger. It is not meant to be a pretty car. It is a useful car. Land-Rovers are used by people who have to drive over rough ground. They are also often used for moving things. The Army uses Land-Rovers, and so do farmers and people who live in rough countryside.

In the duck pond

The eight reindeer who draw the present-laden sledge of St Nicholas (Santa Claus) are: Blitzen, Comet, Cupid, Dancer, Dasher, Donner, Prancer and Vixen.

It takes just over eight minutes for a ray of light to reach us from the Sun, and four and a half years for a similar beam to reach Earth from Proxima Centauri, the next nearest star.

On 1 July 1969, Queen Elizabeth II invested Prince Charles as Prince of Wales; it was his future wife Diana's eighth birthday.

SNAIL COMES LAST

ASPIRE

CLARIFY
CLASP

DAILY

ECLIPSE

LEARN
LEAST
LINKAGE

MARAUD
MATADOR
MISJUDGE

NEVER
NURTURE

PAUPER
PIGEON
PLANS
PRISM

ROUGH

SARONG
SAUNA
SEDAN
SNAIL

N	A	D	E	S	P	I	L	C	E
O	H	E	A	C	L	E	A	R	N
E	M	G	L	C	A	T	I	V	Y
G	I	A	U	S	N	P	N	L	P
I	S	K	T	O	S	U	I	A	G
P	J	N	M	A	R	A	U	D	N
R	U	I	A	T	D	P	U	E	O
I	D	L	U	I	E	O	V	N	R
S	G	R	O	R	L	E	R	E	A
M	E	Y	F	I	R	A	L	C	S

Clue: Musical term (6 letters)

NINE LITTLE MEN

These nine little men look alike, but one is slightly different from the others. Can you spot him?

STUPID SID IS SO THICK THAT WHEN HE WENT TO SEE A MIND-READER, HE GOT HIS MONEY BACK!

BLANK

What happens when a witch loses her temper?
She flies off the handle.

Knock! Knock!
Who's there?
Scott.
Scott who?
Scott egg all over his shirt.

Infant school boy: I couldn't get to sleep last night Miss.
Teacher: Did you try counting sheep?
Boy: Yes Miss. But it didn't work.
Teacher: Why not.
Boy: Well I can only count up to six, can't I.

Doctor, doctor, I think I'm shrinking.
You'll just have to be a little patient.

Teacher: Has anyone in this class ever been troubled with appendicitis?
Alec: Only when I have to spell it.

What's black, white and impossible?
An 'A' level history paper.

Knock, knock.
Who's there?
Carlotta.
Carlotta who?
Car lot a use with no wheels!

Father: Don't forget it's your mother's birthday next week, son.
Son: I won't, Dad.
Father: When I forgot it was awful.
Son: What did she say?
Father: Nothing. For two weeks.

Knock, knock.
Who's there?
Royce.
Royce who?
Royce pudding or semolina?

'Ann,' said the dancing mistress. 'There are two things stopping you becoming the world's greatest ballerina.
'What are they, Miss?' asked Ann.
'Your feet.'

Teacher: Alec! I asked you to write an essay about milk and you've only written three lines.
Alec: Yes Miss. I've written about condensed milk.

Alec: 'Dad just bought a baby car.'
Friend: 'What do you mean?'
Alec: 'It won't go anywhere without a rattle.'

What runs around all day and lies down at night with its tongue hanging out?
A training shoe.

Nudists are people who wear one-button suits.

'What did you have for lunch at school today?'
'Gegs.'
'What's gegs.'
'Scrambled eggs.'

Knock, knock.
Who's there?
Canoe.
Canoe who?
Canoe help me with my homework, please, Dad. I'm stuck.

Waiter, is there egg custard on the menu?
Not now, sir, I've wiped it off.

'How old were you on your last birthday, Alec?'
'Ten, Sir.'
'And how old will you be on your next birthday?'
'Twelve, Sir.'
'That's impossible Alec.'
'No, Sir. It's my eleventh birthday today.'

What's white outside, black inside and wriggles about?
A cockroach sandwich.

Knock, knock.
Who's there?
Sabina.
Sabina who?
Sabina long time since you were at school Alec. Are you feeling better?

WHHHAAART ??

Science teacher: Alec! Do you remember that yesterday we were talking about what foods are good for you.
Alec: Yes Sir!
Teacher: Well how do we know that carrots are good for our eyes?
Alec: Because we never see rabbits wearing glasses.

What did the ghost play on the piano?
A haunting tune.

MR. MACBRAGGLE

Maths teacher: Alec! If tomatoes were 80p a pound and you had £2.40, how many would you buy.
Alec: None, Sir. If I had £2.40, I'd go to the pictures.

First skeleton: Brr, it's cold today.
Second skeleton: Yes, that wind's blowing right through me.

What do you call a man sitting in a pile of autumn leaves?
Russel.

There once was a schoolboy named Sid,
Who ate ten Mars Bars for a quid.
When asked, 'Are you faint?'
He said, 'No I ain't.
But I don't feel as well as I did.'

Knock, knock.
Who's there?
Dora.
Dora who?
Dora funny face on the blackboard.

What do you call a reptile that suffers from seasickness?
An illigator.

Doctor, doctor, I think I've been bitten by a vampire!
Drink this glass of water.
Will it make me better?
No, but I'll be able to see if your neck leaks.

What creature eats faster than any other creature?
A goblin.

Alec: I eaten seven hamburgers for lunch, Miss.
Teacher: Ate, Alec! Ate!
Alec: No Miss, seven. There were eight on the plate but I couldn't manage the last one.

Janitor: I'll teach you to break the school windows.
Alec: Oh good! I've been trying all morning and only broken one so far.

Knock! Knock!
Who's there?
Victor.
Victor who?
Victor his trousers climbing over the gate.

Biology teacher: Alec, name me three bears.
Alec: Mummy Bear, Daddy Bear and Baby Bear.

Teacher: Give me a sentence using the word 'urchin'.
Lucy: Please, miss, 'Urchin was so pointed it almost met 'er nose.'

UP IN THE AIR

STAND IN A DOORWAY, AND PRESS THE BACK OF YOUR WRISTS AGAINST THE FRAME AS HARD AS YOU CAN...

AFTER A MINUTE, STEP INTO THE ROOM, AND...

'HEY PRESTO!' — YOUR ARMS WILL FLOAT UPWARDS !!

wonder if it works with paws?

IT'S IMPOSSIBLE!

Stand with your right side and right foot against a wall...

Now lift your left leg...

Pick yourself up and try again... and again... and again..!!

IT'S IMPOSSIBLE !!

WALKING STICKS ARE NOT ALLOWED!

DID YOU HEAR ABOUT THE EMPTY SLEEVES?

YES — THEY WERE QUITE 'ARMLESS!

40

¹ Y	² L	³ K	⁴ S	⁵ W	⁶ L	⁷ G
⁸ K	⁹ A	¹⁰ R	¹¹ W	¹² O	¹³ T	¹⁴ O
¹⁵ S	¹⁶ L	¹⁷ L	¹⁸ A	¹⁹ I	²⁰ F	²¹ O
²² N	²³ O	²⁴ W	²⁵ S	²⁶ W	²⁷ E	²⁸ S
²⁹ I	³⁰ B	³¹ O	³² N	³³ I	³⁴ L	³⁵ W FINISH
³⁶ O	³⁷ W	³⁸ R	³⁹ N	⁴⁰ E	⁴¹ T	⁴² A
⁴³ R	⁴⁴ C	⁴⁵ K	⁴⁶ O	⁴⁷ O	⁴⁸ H	⁴⁹ D
⁵⁰ G	⁵¹ P	⁵² I	⁵³ E	⁵⁴ R	⁵⁵ E	⁵⁶ K
⁵⁷ A	⁵⁸ M	⁵⁹ H	⁶⁰ S	⁶¹ O	⁶² R	⁶³ C
⁶⁴ T START	⁶⁵ H	⁶⁶ R	⁶⁷ U	⁶⁸ N	⁶⁹ J	⁷⁰ A

FOLLOW THE BIRDS

PASS THROUGH EACH SQUARE ONCE ONLY TO SPELL OUT THIRTEEN BIRDS.

9

The ninth most intelligent animal is the pig.

The ancient city of Troy was rebuilt nine times.

All vessels afloat on the high seas carry code books of the international signals printed in nine languages.

It is possible to win a 501-up game of darts with just nine throws: seven treble 20s, a treble 15 and a double 18.

Did you hear about...

...the stupid hitch-hiker who set out early to miss the traffic?

10

Ten litres (18 pt) of cream are needed to make 450 g (1 lb) of butter.

Queen Elizabeth II keeps ten corgi dogs.

The lowest number which can be divided exactly by all the numbers 1 to 10 is 2,520.

Ten times as many men as women are colour-blind.

Limerick Fun

Quicksands burp and bubble,
Better cross them at the double;
If not, you see,
You soon will be
Up to your neck in trouble.

There was a young lady called Pat
Who sat with a cat on a mat
When along came a Puma –
An over-consumer –
That was the end of the mat, the cat and Pat!

For his wedding, a very late suitor
Rode into church on his scooter.
He knocked down the Dean,
And said, 'Sorry old bean,
I ought to have sounded my hooter.'

There once was a writer named Wright,
Who instructed his son to write right.
He said, 'Son, write Wright right.
It is not right to write
Wright as 'rite' – try to write Wright aright!'

An old lady who lived by the park
Is burgled a lot after dark.
Her dog's an old pet,
But she really should get
Another that can at least bark.

There was a young girl called Joni,
Who ate plates of boiled macaroni.
She got very fat,
But she didn't mind that,
'Cos she bounced when she fell off her pony.

The monster from Mars is quite horrid:
His clothes are ill-cut and so florid,
His legs number three,
I'm glad he's not me –
His face has no nose and no forehead.

TRIPLETS

Three of the eight pictures are identical in every detail. Can you spot the triplets?

FLOWER ARRANGEMENTS

THE PICTURE CLUES SHOULD REMIND YOU OF FLOWERS. CAN YOU REMEMBER THEM?

// Finish the words \\

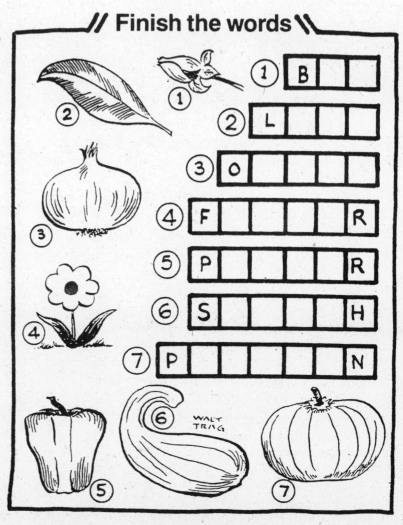

1. B ☐ ☐ ☐
2. L ☐ ☐ ☐ ☐
3. O ☐ ☐ ☐ ☐ ☐
4. F ☐ ☐ ☐ ☐ R
5. P ☐ ☐ ☐ ☐ R
6. S ☐ ☐ ☐ ☐ ☐ H
7. P ☐ ☐ ☐ ☐ ☐ ☐ N

WHEN WAS NAPOLEON BORN?

ON HIS BIRTHDAY!

OLD CROCKS

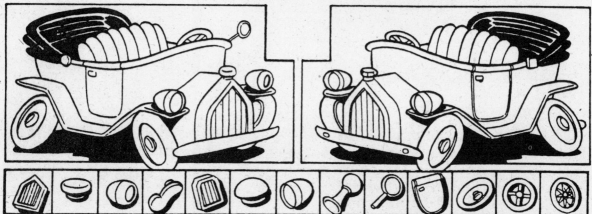

A. Take a good look at these two old crocks. They are different in 10 details. Can you spot them?

B. Five of the spare parts illustrated in the small boxes would not actually be of any use to either car. Which 5 are they?

CLOCK PATIENCE

A CARD GAME FOR ONE PLAYER

ARRANGE THE CARDS IN THIRTEEN PILES OF FOUR AND LAY THEM OUT IN A CIRCLE WITH ONE PILE IN THE MIDDLE. EACH PILE IN THE CIRCLE REPRESENTS A NUMBER ON A CLOCK FACE.

TAKE THE TOP CARD FROM THE CENTRE PILE AND PUT IT IN THE RELEVANT PLACE — AN ACE GOES AT 'ONE', THE JACK AT 'ELEVEN', THE QUEEN AT 'TWELVE', AND SO ON. THEN TAKE A CARD FROM THAT PILE AND SO ON UNTIL ALL THE CARDS ARE FACE UP AROUND THE CLOCK.

BUT... IF YOU TURN OVER A KING, IT GOES ALONGSIDE THE CENTRE PILE AND WHEN THERE ARE NO MORE CARDS IN THE CENTRE PILE TO TURN UP, YOU'RE BEATEN. NO CHEATING NOW!

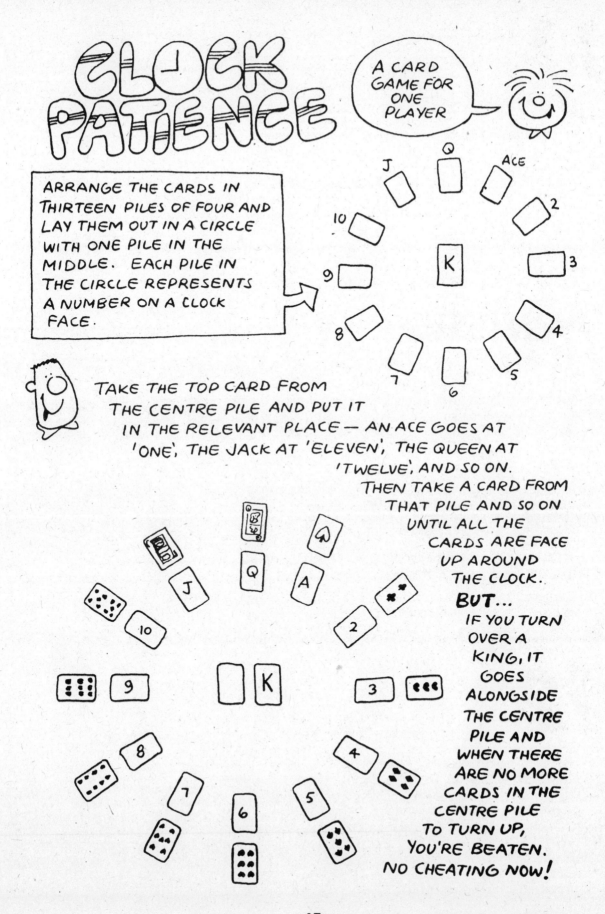

11

The diameter of the planet Jupiter, the biggest in the solar system, is eleven times that of Earth.

In Australia there are eleven sheep for every person.

The ill-fated Dutch artist, Vincent van Gogh (1853–90), produced eleven self-portraits. In London's Courtauld Institute is the famous one with the bandaged ear.

PAINTERS

R	E	E	M	R	E	V	O	L	G
B	O	T	T	I	C	E	L	L	I
R	I	W	E	B	S	T	E	R	B
U	G	A	L	G	G	K	A	O	R
E	G	T	N	A	I	C	N	B	A
G	E	T	A	U	N	Y	S	I	B
H	R	E	I	G	B	D	O	N	A
E	R	A	T	U	R	N	S	S	Z
L	O	U	I	I	L	A	D	O	O
O	C	U	T	N	G	V	H	N	N

BOTTICELLI   ROBINSON
BRABAZON   ROWLANDSON
BRUEGHEL

CORREGGIO   TITIAN

DALI   VAN DYCK
              VERMEER

GAUGUIN   WATTEAU
GLOVER   WEBSTER

Clue: He painted "Blue Boy" (12 letters)

12

A skilled juggler can throw and catch up to twelve balls, hoops or clubs together.

Twelve Americans have walked on the moon: Messrs Armstrong, Aldrin, Conrad, Bear, Shepard, Mitchell, Scott, Irwin, Young, Duke, Cernan and Schmitt – all between 1969 and 1972.

The longest railway tunnel in the world, the Simplon, which links Switzerland and Italy, is just over 12 miles (19 km) long.

ODD SHAPE

How many times does the odd shape appear in the box?

ONE TRAIL LEADS TO THE FARMER'S COW!

Hickory-dickory-dock,
The mouse ran up the clock.
From deep inside
A cuckoo cried:
'At least you ought to knock.'

There's a woman in London called Gertie,
Who's just reached the prime age of thirty
Without using soap –
Unlike you, I hope.
That Gertie is – *phew* – really dirty!

We have an intelligent cat,
Who refuses to hunt mouse or rat.
She'll lie still and wait
For food on her plate;
Now who can blame her for that?

There was a young man from Bengal,
Who was asked to a fancy-dress ball.
He said he would risk it
And went as a biscuit –
But a dog ate him up in the hall!

There was a young girl named Jill
Who said to Jack, 'You're quite ill!
It's so absurd,
Who ever heard
Of a well on the top of a hill?'

I know a girl called Ada,
Who says it's never paid 'er
To put coins in slots,
As not one of her shots
Has brought down a Space Invader.

There was a young lady called Jane,
Who was dreadfully sick on a train.
Not once, but again
And again and again –
And again and again and again.

47

PARTY PLACE SETTINGS

Find a picture of a clown, an astronaut, or anything else you think your friends like, and cut them out carefully.   Paste them onto a sheet of card and cut out the the silhouettes as tidily as possible.

Now collect as many postcards as you have people coming to your party, and fold them in half lengthways.

Put the silhouettes on the card with the head right at the fold, and trace an outline.

Very carefully cut around the outline through both pieces of card but <u>don't cut across the fold</u>.

DAVID

Draw in the details and print one guest's name on each place setting.

13

Triskaidekaphobia is the fear of the number 'thirteen'. American hotels rarely have a Room or Floor 13 preferring the term 12b.

The human body requires regular small amounts of thirteen different minerals in order to function well.

In the centre of a chessboard a bishop can command thirteen squares along the diagonals, but from the sides only seven – worth remembering!

Limerick Fun

Our dog, a Labrador,
Occupies half of the floor.
He's getting so fat
He covers his mat,
Most of the carpet and more!

There was a young man named Ron,
But nobody knows where he's gone.
He sat on this chair,
Now he's simply not there;
Well, it did have a rocket strapped on!

There was a young man of Devizes
Whose appearance was full of surprises:
His nose was askew,
Only one eye was blue,
And his ears were quite different sizes!

In Cardiff, an aircraft designer
Took off in the lightest air liner;
But easterly gales
Swept across Wales,
And took him to North Carolina.

A cheerful old bear at the zoo
Could always find something to do.
If it bored him to go
On a walk to and fro,
He'd turn round and walk fro and to.

There was a bus driver, Rebecca,
Who came to be known as a wrecker.
When a bridge was too low,
She changed at one blow
From a double to a single-decker.

There was a young girl called Poppy
Who wore a hat far too floppy.
When it was in place
It quite hid her face –
Which wasn't necessarily a bad thing!

BIG FAMILIES

A single fly lays eggs four times during the summer, and about 60 eggs at each laying. If nature did not intervene, a fly would generate a family of over a million members during the course of one summer alone.

CHEF PUZZLE

THIS CHEF HAS SOME MIXED-UP LABELS IN HIS KITCHEN. CAN YOU IDENTIFY THEM?

1. rasug
2. tasl
3. erpepp
4. radtsum
5. alasd gniserds

Knock, knock.
Who's there?
Moira.
Moira who?
Moiracles do happen.

Why did Alec take a ladder to school?
Because it was his first day at high school.

Knock, knock.
Who's there?
Nelly.
Nelly who?
Nelly midnight, Cinderella.

My Auntie's gone on holiday to the West
Indies.
Jamaica?
No, she wanted to go.

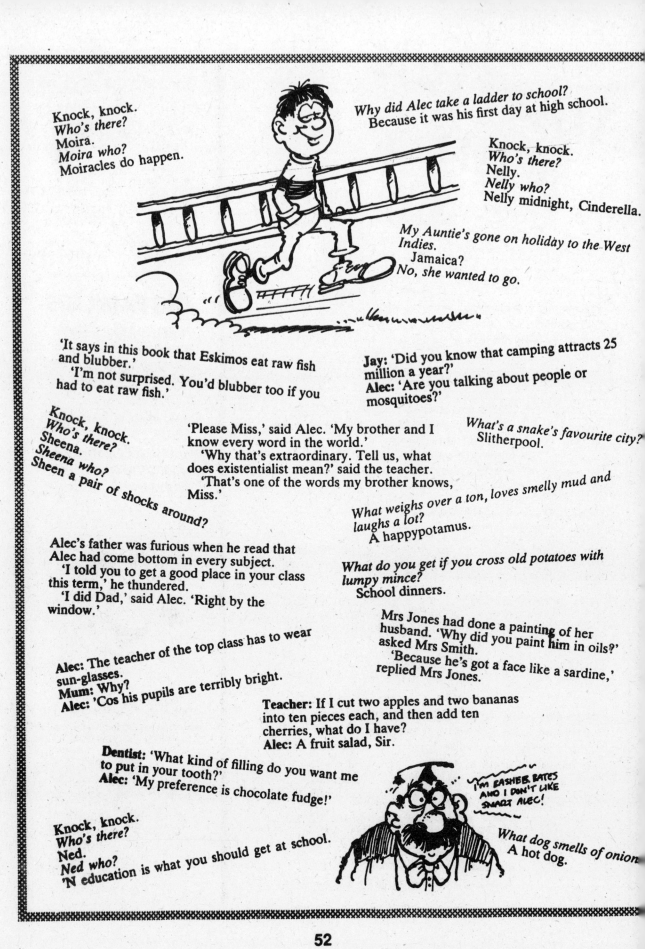

'It says in this book that Eskimos eat raw fish
and blubber.'
'I'm not surprised. You'd blubber too if you
had to eat raw fish.'

Jay: 'Did you know that camping attracts 25
million a year?'
Alec: 'Are you talking about people or
mosquitoes?'

Knock, knock.
Who's there?
Sheena.
Sheena who?
Sheen a pair of shocks around?

'Please Miss,' said Alec. 'My brother and I
know every word in the world.'
'Why that's extraordinary. Tell us, what
does existentialist mean?' said the teacher.
'That's one of the words my brother knows,
Miss.'

What's a snake's favourite city?
Slitherpool.

What weighs over a ton, loves smelly mud and
laughs a lot?
A happypotamus.

Alec's father was furious when he read that
Alec had come bottom in every subject.
'I told you to get a good place in your class
this term,' he thundered.
'I did Dad,' said Alec. 'Right by the
window.'

What do you get if you cross old potatoes with
lumpy mince?
School dinners.

Mrs Jones had done a painting of her
husband. 'Why did you paint him in oils?'
asked Mrs Smith.
'Because he's got a face like a sardine,'
replied Mrs Jones.

Alec: The teacher of the top class has to wear
sun-glasses.
Mum: Why?
Alec: 'Cos his pupils are terribly bright.

Teacher: If I cut two apples and two bananas
into ten pieces each, and then add ten
cherries, what do I have?
Alec: A fruit salad, Sir.

Dentist: 'What kind of filling do you want me
to put in your tooth?'
Alec: 'My preference is chocolate fudge!'

Knock, knock.
Who's there?
Ned.
Ned who?
'N education is what you should get at school.

What dog smells of onion?
A hot dog.

English teacher: Alec! What do you know about famous nineteenth-century writers?
Alec: They're all dead, Miss.

'And what's Alec going to be when he passes his exams?' someone asked his father.
'About 42 I should think.'

Father: 'What did I say I'd do to you if you ate your mother's Christmas pudding?'
Alec: 'Gee Dad, my memory's as bad as yours. I can't remember either!'

What do skunks have that no other animals have?
Baby skunks.

What do you call a man sitting on the doorstep?
Mat.

What cheese is made backwards?
Edam.

What's the difference between a railway guard and a teacher?
One minds the train, the other trains the mind.

'Now remember boys and girls,' said the science teacher. 'You can tell a tree's age by counting the rings in a cross section. One ring for each year.'
Alec went home for tea and found a Swiss Roll on the table.
'I'm not eating that, Mum,' he said. 'It's five years old.'

'You've written in this essay that the Romans wore glasses, Alec. They weren't invented till long after Roman times.'
'But Sir,' said Alec. 'You said last week that on public holidays, the Romans put on lavish spectacles.'

What's a ghost's favourite party game?
Haunt and seek.

What time of year is it when you sit on a pin?
Spring.

Knock, knock.
Who's there?
Evelyn.
Evelyn who?
Evelyn all!

'What can a busy gardener always grow?'
'Tired!'

Mother: 'Did you thank Mrs Smith for inviting you to the party?'
Alec: 'No — the boy before me thanked her and Mrs Smith said, "Don't mention it." So I didn't.'

Headmaster: Alec! You should have been here half an hour ago.
Alec: Why? What happened?

What happened when a skunk did a bank robbery?
The police were soon on the scent.

What happens to wasps that are sick?
They're taken to waspital.

...the man who wanted to go water-skiing, but couldn't find a lake with a slope?

HOW DO YOU MAKE A PIPE LIGHTER?

TAKE THE TOBACCO OUT.

LEFT AND RIGHT

FIND 2 PAIRS OF MITTENS, IT MUST BE ONE FOR EACH HAND.

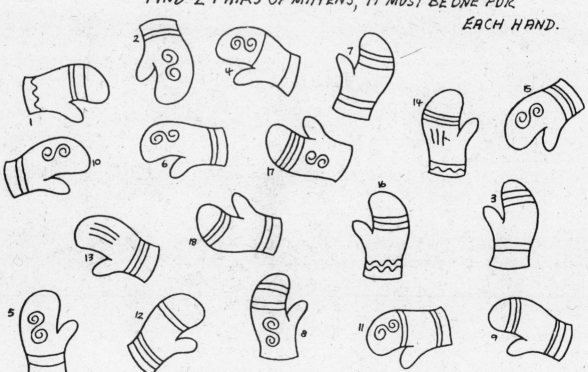

54

14

With about 56 million inhabitants, the UK is the world's fourteenth most populated nation.

In 1063 the River Thames froze over for fourteen days.

14 July is a festive day all over France. It is the anniversary of the storming of the Bastille by the people of Paris during the Revolution of 1789. As it turned out, the Bastille contained only seven prisoners.

A PUZZLE FOR SID...

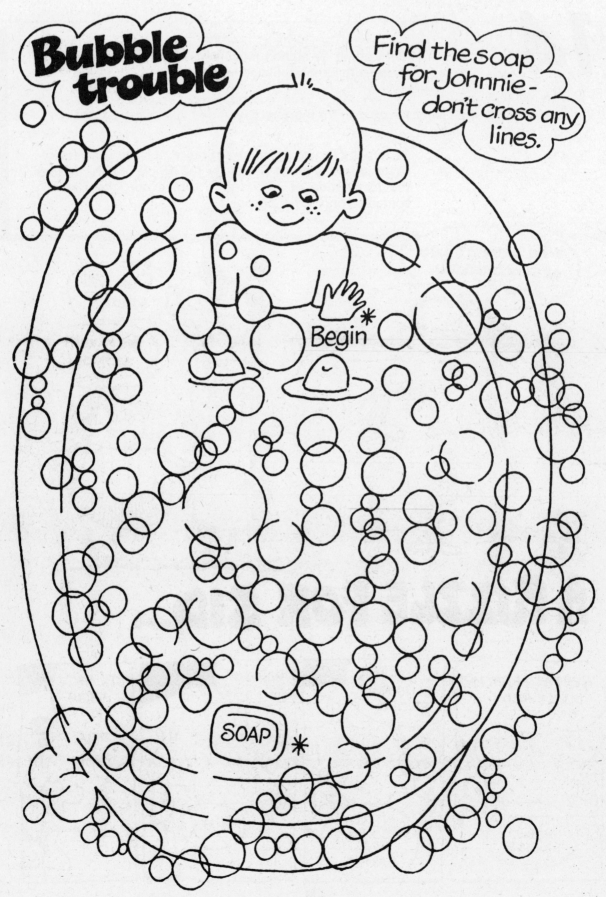

Let's draw a
YACHT WITH SPINNAKER

For a long time, sailing boats were used only for war and trade. Then the Dutch built yachts for pleasure sailing. They gave King Charles II of England a yacht in 1660. He built his own yacht named 'Jamie' and raced it against the Duke of York in 1662.

Today there are lots of different types of yachts. Some have only one sail and one man. Others have lots of sails and up to twenty crew members. Some have a sail called a spinnaker. It has three points. One point is attached to the mast and the other two to the ends of a pole across the front of the yacht. It is used when the wind is behind the yacht to catch the wind. It helps the yacht go even faster.

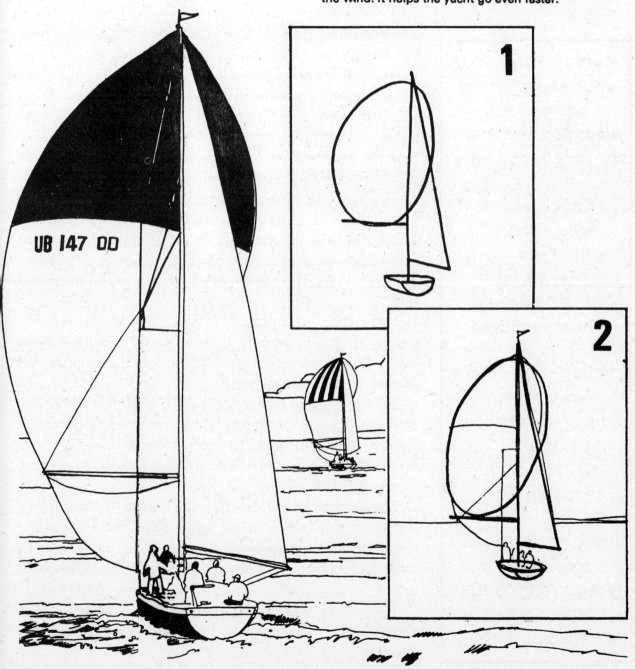

UB 147 OD

1

2

Village of Fear

**It was just a little country village,
but the people seemed different somehow...**

by Gavin Kier

Mother: You've put your shoes on the wrong feet.
Alec: But these are the only feet I have.

Knock, knock.
Who's there?
Fred.
Fred who.
Fred this needle –
I'm cross-eyed.

What's the most important chemistry lesson, Alec?
Never lick the spoon, Sir.

You're so cold-blooded, if a mosquito bit you it would die of pneumonia!

Soon be there, thought Mark Lewis. His car rumbled over the bumpy country road. A nice quiet holiday in a nice quiet English village, he said to himself.

He was looking forward to his few days' holiday with his friend. It would take his mind off his hands. He gripped the steering wheel with the lightest possible touch. He knew that the slightest pressure from his black-gloved hands would buckle and crush the wheel.

This amazing strength was part of an accident involving a new material. Mark had worked in a scientific institute. There had been an accident. To save valuable equipment and a fellow worker's life he had dragged away a container of active waste. He sealed it in a safety room and staggered out.

He awoke in hospital to find his hands horribly mutilated. It was thought that he would never use them again. But when he left hospital he found his hands had acquired a fantastic strength.

For the next few weeks he had to learn to control this strength. At first the things he tried to hold all crumbled. Finally he had managed to control this. But, as his hands were still terribly scarred and mutilated, he always wore skin-tight black gloves.

The car climbed a steep hill. From the top Mark could see the roofs of houses. The car rolled down the hill. On the outskirts of the village Mark noticed an old road leading to what looked like some disused mine workings. He drove on.

The village was quieter than he had expected. There were no cars moving about, just one or two parked here and there.

From the directions his friend Bob Davies had given, Mark was able to find the house easily.

He knocked on the door but there was no reply. He knocked again, louder this time . . . but still no reply.

Strange, thought Mark. I mentioned in my letter when I would be arriving.

Rather than sit in the car, Mark decided to have a look around. He set off. There were not many people about, but those he met stared at him as he passed. He stopped to

Knock, knock.
Who's there?
Lydia.
Lydia who?
Lid o' yer teapot's cracked.

59

admire a small garden that encircled a War Memorial. Then he watched a family of swans glide lazily up the river. Peaceful scenes on a lovely sunny day; but Mark was puzzled. He had an uneasy feeling that everything was too quiet, too still. He looked at his watch and discovered that he'd been away for forty-five minutes. He quickly retraced his steps and as he came in sight of the house, he saw Bob. He went up to him.

"Bob," he said, "where have you been? Didn't you get my letter?"

Mark broke off.

Bob was looking at him blankly. "Who are you?" he asked.

Mark shook him gently. "Bob!" he said. "Don't you know me? You invited me here for a few days."

The puzzled look left Bob's face. "Why, Mark!"

"I called for you about an hour ago," said Mark. "Where were you?"

"I was . . ." Bob paused. "I don't know. I just don't know!"

The two friends went up to Bob's house. Bob brought out his door key. He opened the door. As he was going in, his wrist caught on the side of the door.

"Blast that thing!" he said. "I don't know why I bought it!"

"What?" asked Mark.

"This thing," said Bob, showing him his wrist.

Around his wrist was a strange orange bracelet.

"I can't get it off," said Bob. "I don't know what came over me. I was walking past the shop when I had the sudden urge to go in and buy it. It went on easily but now I can't get the catch to work."

"Go back to the shop," said Mark. "Maybe they can do something."

"I'll fix a meal first," said Bob. Over the meal, the two friends chatted pleasantly.

"Are you going to that shop?" asked Mark, when they had finished eating.

"Yes," said Bob. "We'll go right away."

They left the house. The shop was just off the main street. Bob and Mark went in. It was small and rather dark.

A man stood at the counter. "Can I help you?" he asked.

"Yes," said Bob, "it's about this wrist thing. I wonder if you could get it off?"

The man looked at the orange bracelet.

"No, I can't," he said. "Once that's on, you can't get it off."

He turned to Mark and said, "You're new here, sir. How would you like one?"

"No, thank you," said Mark.

"You can have one for nothing," said the man, "seeing that you are a friend of Mr Davies."

"No, thank you," said Mark again.

They turned to go. The man went over to his counter and pushed a small button underneath. As Mark grasped the door handle, a strange sensation shot through him. He couldn't move. It lasted only a few seconds, but when it ceased he was wearing one of the orange bracelets!

Knock, knock
Who's there?
Norman.
Norman who?
Norman service will be resumed shortly.

I'm as fit as a fiddle.
You look more like a cello.

Which airline do fleas fly on?
British Hair Ways.

What's grey and red all over?
An embarrassed elephant.

Knock, knock.
Who's there?
Israel.
Israel who?
Is rail quicker than road travel?

Knock, knock.
Who's there?
Val.
Val who?
Val, you ought to know by now.

The man was backing away from him saying, "Thank you for changing your mind, sir."

Mark put two fingers round the strange bracelet. He pressed it. It cracked open and fell off.

"No, thank you," he said.

The two men left the shop. They did not see the man scuttle away to the room at the back of the shop and speak into some sort of transmitter.

How do you stop a ten-ton elephant from charging? Take away its credit cards.

When's the best time to buy chicks? When they're going cheep.

What happened when the monster lost a hand? He went to the second-hand shop.

What are assets? Little donkeys.

Is your horse well behaved? Yes. When he comes to a fence he stops and lets me go over first!

Husband: What would you like for Christmas?
Wife: Make it a surprise.
Husband: Right. Boo!!!

"New subject has rejected the control device. Will immobilize his transport and bring him to be examined!"

The two men arrived back at the house.

"What happened in that shop?" asked Mark. "How did he get that bracelet on me?"

"I don't know," replied Bob with a blank look. "I just remember you having it on!"

"Shall I take yours off?" asked Mark.

"Yes," said Bob. "It's beginning to get on my nerves!"

Mark broke off the bracelet.

"Thanks," said Bob. "I feel as if a cloud has been lifted from my mind!"

"I noticed that a few other people in the village wear them," said Mark.

"A few!" exclaimed Bob. "You mean only a few *don't* wear them!"

"I'm puzzled about that shop," said Mark. "I wish I knew how I got that bracelet on!"

"It's the same feeling I had when I met you this afternoon," said Bob.

Nothing happened for the rest of the afternoon. It was in the late evening when things began to happen.

"I thought I heard someone round the back," said Bob.

"I didn't hear anything," said Mark.

"I'm going to see," said Bob, leaving the room.

He was gone a good five minutes when Mark began to be concerned. He too left the room. Bob was not around. The back door was open. Darkness was beginning to fall.

"Bob," said Mark. "Are you there?"

There was no reply. Mark turned from the back door. Then he saw Bob. He was lying in a corner of the kitchen. Mark went over to him. He was unconscious.

Then, without any warning, an arm circled round Mark's throat. Mark was flattened out on the floor. He caught a glimpse of his attacker — it was the owner of the shop! Mark rolled across the floor. The man lunged at him but missed.

Mark tried to get up but the man grabbed his leg. Before he knew what was going on, he was flung through the air and came crashing up against the wall. Through his dazed vision, he could see the man advancing. Mark's hands groped along the skirting board until they came to an electric socket. The man was about to bend over him. Mark dug his fingers into the plaster and pulled the socket out. He exposed bare wires as the man came down. Then he thrust them at the man's chest. There was crackling followed by a flash. The man gave a scream as smoke rose from his clothing. He staggered back and crumpled to the floor.

Mark got up. His amazing hands had saved his life.

Mark let the smoke clear then went over to the man. What he saw amazed him; there were no human features

<hr>

Knock, knock.
Who's there?
Mary.
Mary who?
Mary Christmas to all our readers.

Knock, knock.
Who's there?
Justin.
Justin who?
Just in time for school.

Where do fleas go in the winter?
Search me!
No thanks.

<hr>

There was a young man of Dumfries
Who had the most knobbly knees.
If he went to the park,
He'd go in the dark,
for dogs often mistook them for trees.

What kind of ghosts haunt hospitals?
Surgical spirits.

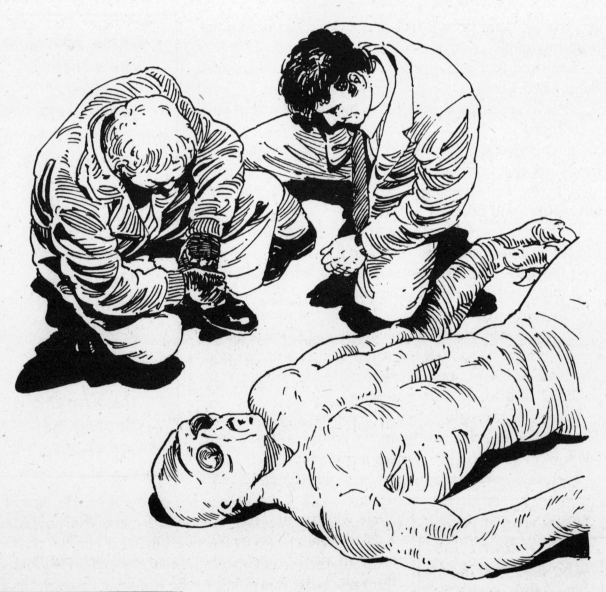

left on the man. His head was large, grey and scaly. Two huge eyes bulged out, lined with veins. At the end of the man's arms were two grey scaly claws.

Bob was back on his feet. "What's that?" he asked.

"I don't know," replied Mark. "It used to be human . . . or was it?"

"It must have grabbed me when I went to check the noise," said Bob.

"Something strange is going on," said Mark. "First these bracelets, now this! Bob, you stay here and get the police!"

"Where are you going?" asked Bob.

"Back to the shop," said Mark, and he was gone.

Mark forced his way into the shop. The door was no problem. He went through into the back of the shop. He turned on the light. There was a strange device on a bench in one corner. Mark went over to it.

Looks like some kind of radio set, he said to himself.

Then he searched through all the drawers, but found nothing. He came to a large cupboard. It was locked. With a swift blow, Mark smashed aside the lock.

The door swung open. This was no ordinary cupboard. Mark saw a flight of old stone steps leading into blackness. He descended.

He was in some sort of tunnel that led away from the shop. Mark pressed on. He went further and further away from the shop. Then the first tunnel seemed to merge with a second.

"Mine workings," said Mark quietly as his hand touched a wooden support.

There was a strange light up ahead. Mark followed it. The blackness was fading now; Mark was bathed in a strange blue light. The sides of the tunnel were propped up with wood, as Mark had felt. There was something up ahead where the tunnel widened out. It looked like some sort of glass case.

As he got closer, Mark saw that it was a huge glass case. Inside was a man – the same man who had attacked him in Bob's kitchen.

Why do you say that Rome must have been built in a night?
I keep hearing people say it wasn't built in a day.

A man with a business in Brecon Is completely unable to reckon. He thinks four plus four Is sixteen or more: His are the bills you should check on!

He was banging on the glass to Mark. "Help!"

Mark couldn't hear a word but he could make that out. He motioned for the man to stand back, then put his fist through the thick, glass-like substance. He smashed a hole large enough for the man to get out.

"Thank heaven!" said the man. "Those things had me in there for days."

"Explain," said Mark.

"My name's Richards," said the man. "I own a small shop in the village. One night I heard a scuffling coming from my cellar. I went down, and they were there! They grabbed me and dragged me to this place. It was all lit up. I was put under a machine with one of them and when I came out, the thing was just like me!"

"You mean those grey creatures?" asked Mark.

"Yes," said Richards. "They were grey. They're down the tunnel . . . that way!" Richards gave a shriek. "Behind you!"

Knock, knock.
Who's there?
Justus.
Justus who?
Just as bad tempered as ever.

Why did the cow jump over the moon?
Because the milkmaid's hands were cold.

65

Mark spun round. Three of the grey creatures were coming up the tunnel. They were armed.

"Run!" said Richards. "Run!"

He turned to run down the tunnel. One of the grey creatures raised his weapon and fired. Richards was enveloped in a green haze, and sank to the ground. The creatures turned to Mark, and he too was caught in the green haze and joined Richards on the ground.

Mark regained consciousness in another glass case. Richards was with him. They were in strange surroundings. There was equipment all around outside the case. Grey creatures worked at the machines. A huge disc-shaped object was in the middle of the machinery.

The two men were wearing the bracelets. A grey creature, larger than the others, was walking in the direction of the case. It stopped outside. Slowly the creature pushed a hidden door, opened it, and stepped in. Richards cowered in fear. "What do you want?" asked Mark.

The creature looked at him for a few moments. Then it spoke. "I am the leader of the people you see before you. We are the people of the Polidons. Soon we will be your masters!"

"What are you doing here?" asked Mark.

"Our planet has been torn apart by warfare," said the creature. "We shall use this planet for our new home!"

"Are you responsible for the bracelets?" asked Mark, holding out his wrist.

"Yes," said the creature. "These have been given to all those in the village above. The people do not know how they got them. The answer lies with us. We used a ray to plant a suggestion in the people's minds to go into the shop and buy one. Our agent was in control of the shop!"

"I'm still puzzled," said Mark.

"I will explain," said the creature. "We captured this man and transformed his features into one of our kind. He went among you humans distributing the bracelets. These bracelets will ensure our control over you humans. I will demonstrate."

The creature produced a small box from a pouch. It worked a dial. Bolts of pain racked through Mark and Richards. The creature turned it off.

"You see," it said. "If we wish, we could black out the village or kill everybody. We are using the village as a place where we can become accustomed to your way of life. Then we will transform the features of all the villagers into our people. We will go out into the world. Then we will rise up and conquer. Our spacecraft is based in these mine workings."

"You are outnumbered," said Mark.

"Our people will spread the bracelets of pain," said the creature. "Nothing can stop us!"

The creature turned and left the glass case. Mark snapped off his bracelet, and freed Richards.

"We'll have to try and escape," he said. "When we get out, you run up the tunnel. I'll get into their spaceship and destroy it!"

Mark prepared his hands for their task. He swung them back and brought them crashing into the side of the case, which splintered and cracked. Mark crashed his fists through again. Then he dived through the hole. Richards followed. The creatures turned towards them. Richards ran for his life, down the tunnel and into the darkness.

Mark made for the huge disc that was the alien spacecraft. There was a ramp leading into the disc. Mark flung himself up it.

Inside was all brightly coloured. A creature approached him. It was unarmed. Mark lashed out and brought the creature crashing to the floor. Another creature, this one armed, arrived from a passageway. Mark grabbed the barrel of the weapon and pulled the creature towards him. He knocked the creature to the floor with a crushing blow. Mark was now armed.

He gunned down two other creatures standing outside a door. Mark kicked the door open. He had hit the jackpot. This was the main control room.

The leader of the creatures was seated in a strange chair. All around him were controls and dials. Other creatures sat at the controls.

"Destroy the human!" screamed the leader.

A creature produced a pistol from below his seat. As he fired, Mark put his hands up to his head. The blast of the pistol was taken on his hands. Searing with pain, Mark directed the gun at the creature. He fired and the creature slumped over his chair.

Mark sprayed the room with a burst of fire. The creatures dropped where they sat. Their controls burst into flames. There was a small explosion, and fragments of metal rained down in the room. The whole spacecraft began to shake.

Mark left the room and ran. He jumped down the ramp. A fire was now raging inside the spacecraft. Mark couldn't go back through the dark tunnel because there were too many creatures.

Mark saw that another tunnel led away from the spacecraft. It was part of the original mine workings. Mark ran for his life. He could hear the tunnel rumbling. Pieces of earth fell in his path.

At last he could feel cold air blowing on him. He staggered out into a starry night. He was at the minehead. There was a tremendous roaring and rumbling from down the tunnel and the whole mine exploded into a mass of flame. Mark was showered with dirt. The countryside was lit up with flame. Then the dirt shower stopped.

Mark stood, watching the flames. The Polidon plan of conquest was over.

Do you have trouble making decisions? Yes and no!

I've got a good idea. Beginner's luck.

What book tells you about chickens? The Hencyclopedia.

What is it that goes 99 plonk?

A centipede with a wooden leg.

Sid puts on a clean pair of socks every day... the only trouble is, by the end of the week, he can't get his shoes on!

ROLAND BUTTER...

...the WACKY WAITER!

WAITER! WHAT'S THIS **LUMP** IN MY GRAVY?

THAT'S NOT A LUMP, SIR— THAT'S YOUR **STEAK!**

WHY DIDN'T YOU GO TO TOMMY'S BIRTHDAY PARTY?

THE INVITATION SAID 7–8, AND I'M ONLY 6.

HOW DO YOU MAKE A JACKET LAST?

MAKE THE TROUSERS FIRST!

SPOT THE DIFFERENCES

Our mad scribbling soccer fan has made six changes to the drawing on the right.
~ Can you spot them?

HOW?

The boy and the dog have agreed that the bone is not to lie between them any longer. Even though they want the bone moved, they have decided it must not be kicked or touched in any way. How then is it to be moved?

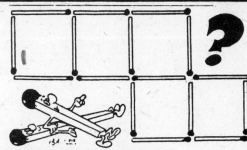

FIVE BECOMES FOUR

Can you change these five squares into four by moving two of the matchsticks?

15

Until it was named after Sir George Everest, Surveyor-General of India 1830–43, the world's highest mountain was known to the English as Peak 15.

The USSR covers 15 per cent of the land surface of the world.

Every 15° longitude represents one hour more or less than Greenwich Mean Time.

MARATHON MATT!

FAT MATT IS ON A SPONSORED RUN — IF HE GETS TWO DOUGHNUTS FOR EVERY BRIDGE HE CROSSES, AND ONE DOUGHNUT FOR EVERY BRIDGE HE RUNS UNDER, HOW MANY WILL HE GET IF HE FINISHES THE COURSE?

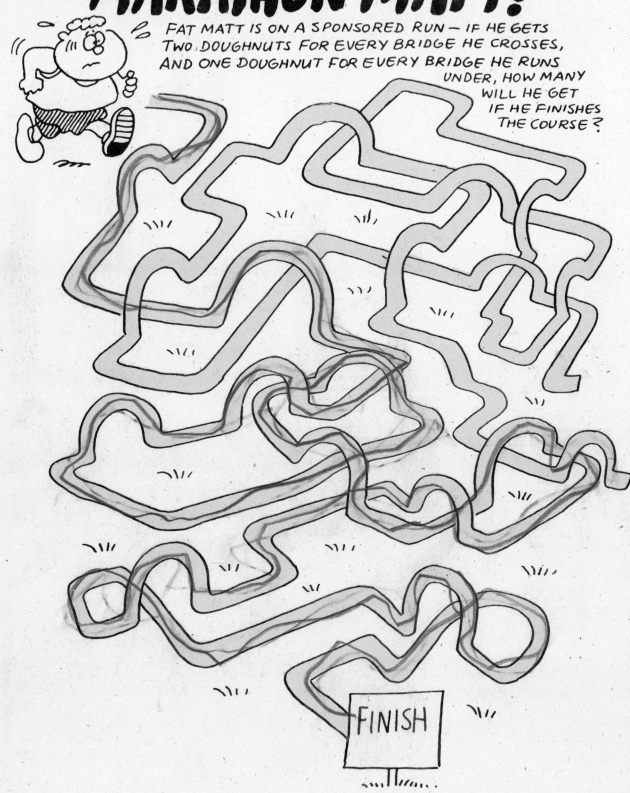

FINISH

16

Astronauts circling the Earth may be able to see sixteen sunrises and sixteen sunsets in every twenty-four hours.

The chrysanthemum, Japan's national flower, introduced into England in 1789, has sixteen petals.

Under Norman rule, the width of a highway was regulated to allow for the passage of two waggons in reverse direction, or of sixteen armour-clad knights riding knee to knee.

CIRCULAR

FIT THE PICTURE NAMES INTO THE CIRCLE.

Reflections...!

The right-hand picture was supposed to be the exact mirrored reflection, however there are five errors. Which?

Sid is so stupid that he went to the dentist to have a wisdom tooth put **in!**

an ENCYCLOPEDIC MEMORY

OF COURSE YOU CAN'T MEMORIZE
EVERY WORD IN A LARGE ENCYCLOPEDIA *
BUT YOU CAN CONVINCE OTHERS THAT YOU
CAN!

FIRST YOU NEED TO DO A LITTLE HOMEWORK.
MARK OUT A SHEET OF PAPER LIKE THIS:

PAGE	COLUMN	LINE DOWN	NUMBER OF WORDS ALONG
99			
198			
297			
396			
495			
594			
693			
792			
891			

NOW GO TO THE
ENCYCLOPEDIA, WHICH SHOULD
HAVE AT LEAST 900 PAGES. FOR EACH OF
THE NINE PAGES, SELECT A COLUMN, A LINE
AND A WORD. IF, FOR EXAMPLE, YOU CHOSE THE
RIGHT HAND COLUMN ON PAGE 495, THE TENTH LINE
DOWN AND THE THIRD WORD ALONG WAS 'RANSOM', YOU'D
FILL IN THE SHEET:

495   R   10   THIRD: RANSOM

HIDE THE SHEET WHERE ONLY YOU CAN SEE IT WHILE YOU DO THE TRICK.

NOW, ASK SOMEONE TO THINK OF A THREE-DIGIT NUMBER IN
WHICH THE THREE DIGITS ARE DIFFERENT, e.g. 692. NEXT, ASK
THEM TO REVERSE THEM (296) AND FINALLY TO SUBTRACT THE
SMALLER FROM THE LARGER (692-296 = 396). THIS
CALCULATION WILL ALWAYS GIVE YOU ONE OF THE PAGE
NUMBERS ON YOUR LIST. GIVE THEM THE ENCYCLOPEDIA
AND TELL THEM TO TURN TO PAGE 396. THEN SAY,
'GO DOWN THE RIGHT HAND COLUMN UNTIL YOU GET
TO THE TWELFTH LINE. THE FOURTH WORD
ALONG IS...'

* IF YOU HAVEN'T GOT AN
ENCYCLOPEDIA,
YOU CAN USE
A BIBLE.

FLOWERS

Arrange the initial letters of the pictures to name five flowers.

LION'S MAZE

The Lion has escaped from his cage. See if you can find which path the Keeper must take to find him again.

IN A QUANDARY

The two gentlemen shown here were taking their dogs for a walk and all was well. But suddenly the dogs started to play and their leads got into an awful tangle. In the end the men couldn't decide which lead led to which dog! Can you help them to sort themselves out?

WHEN IS IT BAD LUCK TO HAVE A BLACK CAT FOLLOW YOU?

WHEN YOU'RE A MOUSE!!

HEH! HEH!

75

1

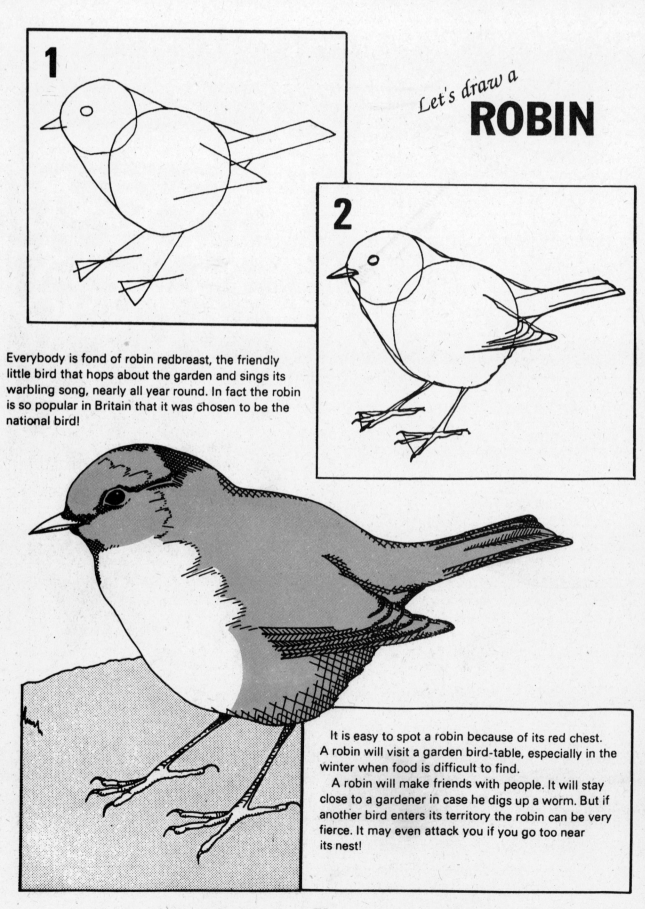

2

Everybody is fond of robin redbreast, the friendly little bird that hops about the garden and sings its warbling song, nearly all year round. In fact the robin is so popular in Britain that it was chosen to be the national bird!

It is easy to spot a robin because of its red chest. A robin will visit a garden bird-table, especially in the winter when food is difficult to find.

A robin will make friends with people. It will stay close to a gardener in case he digs up a worm. But if another bird enters its territory the robin can be very fierce. It may even attack you if you go too near its nest!

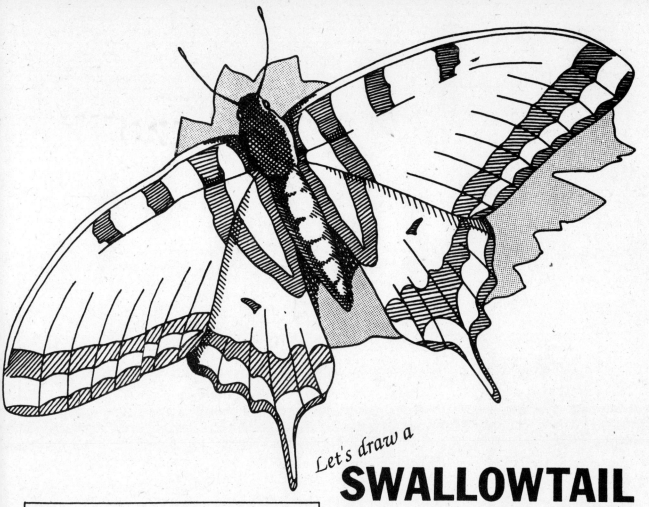

Let's draw a

SWALLOWTAIL

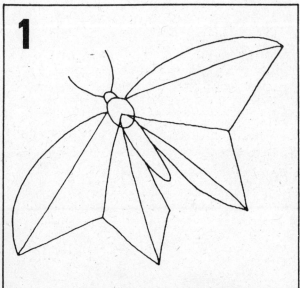

This butterfly is very colourful. It is yellow and black with some blue marks and two bright red patches on the inside of its hindwings. The caterpillar is even more colourful: it is bright green with orange and black stripes.

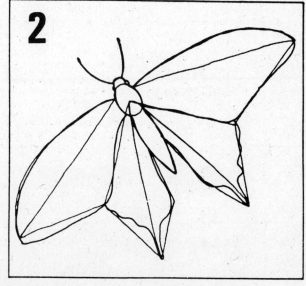

It gets its name because its hindwings end in points—rather like a swallow's tail. It lives on the Norfolk Broads. The eggs are laid on milk parsley, but the caterpillar also feeds on fennel and wild carrot. It is quite large for a British butterfly and its wings can be up to nine centimetres across.

17

There are seventeen letters in Featherstonehaugh, the longest unhyphenated surviving English surname. It is pronounced 'Fanshaw'.

The Sahara Desert averages seventeen days of rain in a year.

The game of soccer (association football) is governed by only seventeen rules.

Limerick Fun

A girl on a train in Florida
Couldn't have been any horrider.
She ate fish and chips,
And spat orange pips
All along the corridor!

There once was a ghost named Paul,
Who went to a fancy-dress ball.
To shock all the guests
He went quite undressed,
But the rest couldn't see him at all!

An artist called Botticelli
Painted a model named Nelly
She slapped him, 'Take that,
You've painted me fat –
I'm slim and I've been on the telly.'

A flea and a fly in a flue,
Were trapped, so they thought, 'What to do?'
'Let us fly,' said the flea,
'Let us flee,' said the fly,
So they flew through a flaw in the flue!

There was a young lady of Riga
Who went for a ride on a tiger.
They returned from the ride
With the lady inside,
And a smile on the face of the tiger.

Have you ever seen a ghost?
I have, while I was eating my toast!
It came through the wall,
Amazing us all,
And said: 'Tell me, which way to the coast?'

A man from Stockton-on-Tees
Produced phenomenal peas.
He then moved to Jarrow
And grew a green marrow
Too big to go in the deep-freeze.

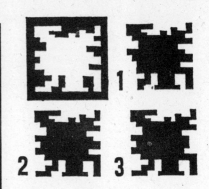

FOUR PATTERNS

At first glance these four figures look exactly alike—apart from the fact that one of them is white and the three others black. One of the black patterns (1 to 3), fits into the white, but which one?

THINK OF A NUMBER

With the help of five matchsticks, as shown in the drawing, it is possible to make the number 141. Now try to make the number 12 with the same amount of matchsticks. Naturally, there's a trick to it.

On the school outing Alec ran short of money and borrowed £5 from the teacher. On the train back home he wanted a hamburger so he borrowed another £1 from her. 'I'll give it back to you tomorrow, promise, Miss.'

The next day he came into school clutching a squid that had a bandage round one of its tentacles.

'Here you are Miss,' he said. 'Here's the sick squid I owe you.'

Knock! Knock!
Who's there?
Euripides.
Euripides who?
Euripides you buy me a new pair.

'That's it. I'm not going back to school,' Alec said after his first day.
'Why ever not?' asked his mum.
'I can't read. I can't spell. And teacher won't let me talk; so what's the point?'

Friend: 'I can lie in bed and watch the sun rise.'
Alec: 'So what? I can sit on a stool and watch the kitchen sink!'

Why was the banker sitting in a tree?
Because he had just been made branch manager.

'Waiter, will my hamburger be long?'
'No, sir, it will be round.'

Alec: 'I'm going to give you a teapot for Christmas.'
Mum: 'But I already have a teapot.'
Alec: 'No you don't, I just dropped it!'

Nurse: The new doctor is really amusing. He'll have you in stitches.
Patient: I hope not. I only came to collect my prescription.

What's a cheerful flea called?
A hoptimist.

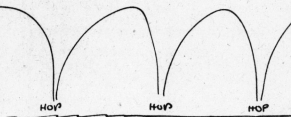

'Alec,' said the geography teacher. 'Tell m two animals that live in Africa.'
'Er . . . the lion.'
'Right. And the second?'
'Another lion, Sir.'

'Jean, define a baby.'
'A soft pink thing that makes a lot of noise at one end and has no sense of responsibility at the other.'

What do short-sighted ghosts wea
Spooktacles.

Teacher: What's HNO_3?
Alec: It's . . . er . . . it's on the tip of my tongue, Sir.
Teacher: Well spit it out at once, it's nitric acid.

Teacher: 'If you had to multiply 327 by 829, what would you get?'
Alec: 'The wrong answer.'

Sally: When I went to the doctor he put me on an olive oil diet.
Susie: Did you lose weight?
Sally: No, but I've stopped squeaking.

Gail: 'Does your mother have an automatic dishwasher?'
Alec: 'Yes, my father.'

Geography teacher: Where are elephants found?
Alec: Elephants are so big, I'm surprised they ever get lost.

Knock! Knock!
Who's there?
Juliet.
Juliet who?
Juliet too much and now she feels sick.

Knock, knock.
Who's there?
Augustine.
Augustine who?
August in Spain is too hot.

'Doctor, doctor! Every time I drink a cup of tea I get a sharp pain in by nose.'
'Have you tried taking the spoon out of the cup?'

What's yellow and extremely stupid?
Thick custard.

What are the best things to put in a Christmas cake?
Your teeth.

Cookery teacher: Alec! How would you make scrambled eggs?
Alec: I'd crack some eggs into a bowl, add a little milk, salt and pepper. Melt some butter in a saucepan and pour the eggs in when it's hot.
Teacher: Well done. What would you do next?
Alec: I'd hold the pan and get three chums to shake the stove.

What happened to Ray when a ten-ton truck ran over him?
He became X-Ray.

What did the strict father ghost say to his son?
Spook only when you are spooken to.

Teacher: If Shakespeare was alive today he'd still be considered a very remarkable man.
Alec: Of course he would. He'd be 450 years old.

'Alec,' said the teacher. 'Suppose you were in the jungle and in the distance you saw a pride of lions coming towards you, what steps would you take?'
'The longest ones possible, Sir.'

Knock, knock.
Who's there?
Mister.
Mister who?
Missed a bus and had to walk.

Alec: 'A girlfriend of mine went on a coconut diet.'
John: 'How much weight did she lose?'
Alec: 'None, but you should see her climb trees!'

Teacher: Who broke that window?
Alec: It was Susan, Miss.
Susan: It wasn't. You threw the brick.
Alec: Yes. But you ducked.

Knock, knock.
Who's there?
Oberon.
Oberon who?
Oberon the other side of the road.

What's black when it's clean and white when it's dirty?
A blackboard.

What's a cannibal's favourite drink?
Wine with a lot of body.

Teacher: 'What is a prickly pear?'
Alec: 'Two porcupines.'

YO-HOO

octor, doctor, what can you give me for
ind?
How about a kite?

KEEPING TOGETHER

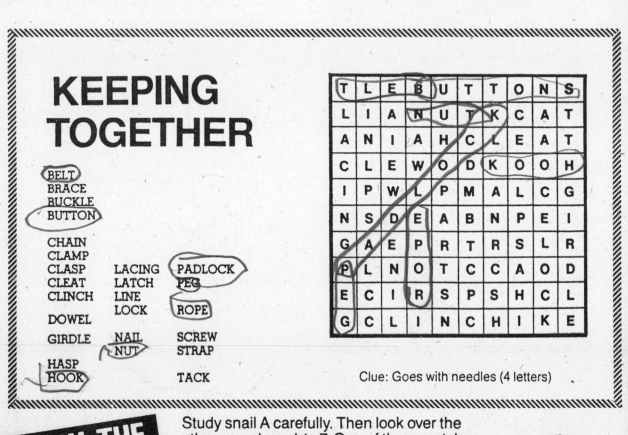

BELT
BRACE
BUCKLE
BUTTON

CHAIN
CLAMP
CLASP   LACING   PADLOCK
CLEAT   LATCH   PEG
CLINCH   LINE
           LOCK   ROPE
DOWEL

GIRDLE   NAIL   SCREW
           NUT   STRAP

HASP
HOOK   TACK

Clue: Goes with needles (4 letters)

MATCH THE SHADOW

Study snail A carefully. Then look over the others numbered 1–7. One of them matches snail A exactly—which?

18

Cats have eighteen toes – five on each of their front feet and four on each of their hind feet. All except cheetahs have sharp, hooked claws, which can be retracted into sheaths.

Thunder can be heard up to 18 miles (29 km) away.

The magnificent thirteenth-century rose window in Notre Dame Cathedral, Paris, has a diameter of 18 m (59 ft).

Puzzle

Find 12 things beginning with P. Find a way between the stars.

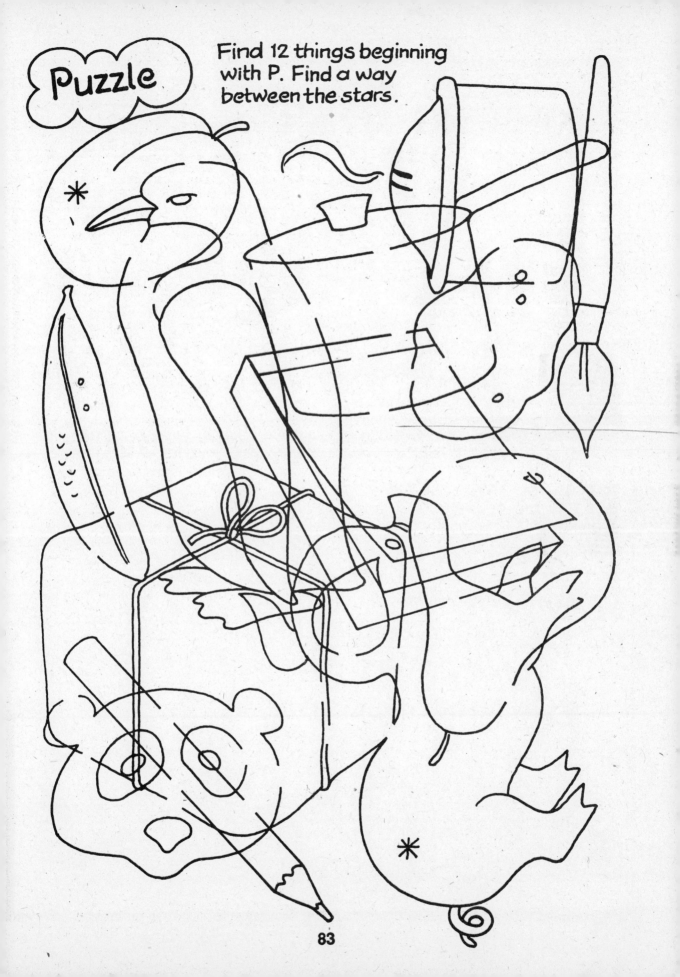

BALLOONS

Without using a pencil, see if you can see which of these three balloons will actually reach the landing target.

TARGET

HOW WAS YOUR FIRST DAY AT SCHOOL JOHNNY?

IT WAS ALL RIGHT EXCEPT FOR SOME BLOKE CALLED SIR WHO KEPT SPOILING ALL THE FUN!!!

A SPOTTY PUZZLE

Can you spot which 2 rows are identical?

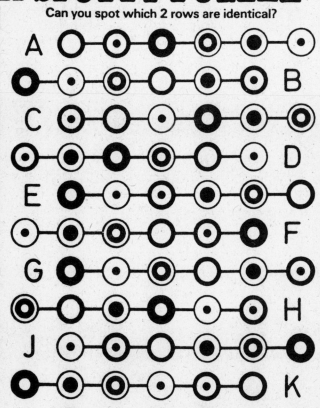

A
B
C
D
E
F
G
H
J
K
L

RHYMING PAIRS

Look at the objects on this page and then pair off those that rhyme.

HOPSCOTCH

YOUR GRANNY PROBABLY REMEMBERS PLAYING HOPSCOTCH. CHALK OUT SQUARES ON A PIECE OF GROUND, LIKE THIS

The first player tries to throw a stone into the first square. If he does, he hops over square ①, into square ②, without landing on the line, turns around to pick up the stone (still standing on one leg) and then hops into each square and back down again. When he gets back to square ②, he chalks his initials in square ①, hops over it and lands back home.

He then tries to throw the stone into square ②, and so on until he has initialled each square.

If the stone doesn't land in the square, or if the hopper lands on a line or trips over, he goes back to the end of the queue to wait for another turn, and the next player gets his shot.

Sid's version →

what game do policemen play?

cop-scotch!

19

Only nineteen minutes after Neil Armstrong stepped on to the Moon's surface on 21 July 1969, he was joined by Edwin 'Buzz' Aldrin.

Nineteen lamps are required to provide the illumination in the massive torch held in the right hand of the Statue of Liberty in New York harbour.

The Earth is lapped by Venus, its nearest planetary neighbour, every nineteen months.

PERSIAN HALF MOONS

These two half moons can be drawn with one single line—that is to say, without having to lift the pencil from the paper. Try to figure out how it is done.

HOW MANY BRICKS?

How many bricks can you see?

Limerick Fun

The conductor of a band
Is perched on a little stand.
It's the musicians who play,
Yet he gets most pay –
Just for waving his hand!

A wonderful bird is the Toucan,
It eats just as much as you can.
Is it able to speak
With food in its beak?
It's said that the one at the zoo can.

There was a young girl called Amba
Who charmed a snake – a mamba.
With a hypnotic glance,
She made the snake dance
To a rhumba, tango and samba.

A driver named Jonathon Master
Stepped on the gas to go faster.
Just for some thrills
He flew over the hills,
And ended in total disaster.

My tortoise, Araminta,
Is really not a sprinter;
She does the crawl
From spring to fall,
Then sleeps all through the winter.

There once was a man with two poodles,
Whose names were Toodles and Doodles.
Their favourite dish
Was not meat or fish;
The poodles loved oodles of noodles!

There once was a bald gorilla
Who, wrapped up in a furry chinchilla,
Escaped from a zoo
Through a gap in the loo,
And now works in a cafe in Manilla.

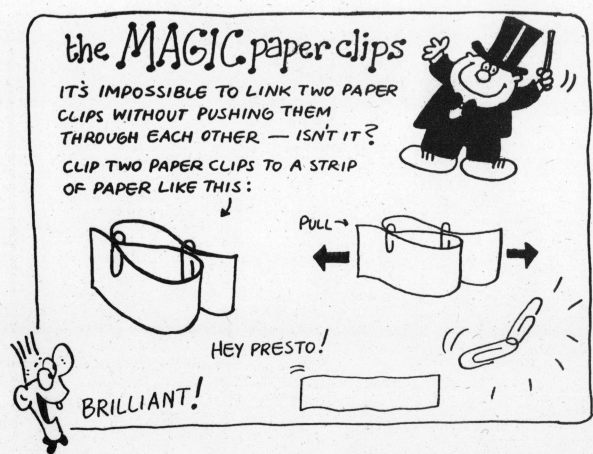

the MAGIC paper clips

IT'S IMPOSSIBLE TO LINK TWO PAPER CLIPS WITHOUT PUSHING THEM THROUGH EACH OTHER — ISN'T IT?

CLIP TWO PAPER CLIPS TO A STRIP OF PAPER LIKE THIS:

PULL →

← →

HEY PRESTO!

BRILLIANT!

ALL JUMBLED UP

If you were to pull the ends of each of these four knots, two would tangle and two would not. Can you tell which ones would tangle and which ones would not?

20

One in every twenty people suffer from seasickness.

Ladybird grubs eat up to twenty greenflies a day.

It is twenty years before an oak tree begins to bear acorns.

Each of a horse's limbs contains twenty bones. **Although its frame is much bigger, a horse – with 205 bones – has one less than a human.**

21

In June 1965, Edward White, an American astronaut engaged on the Gemini IV mission, free-floated outside his spacecraft for about twenty-one minutes.

François Mitterand (born 1916) became twenty-first President of France in May 1981.

Mary Wollstonecroft Shelley (1797–1851) was twenty-one when she wrote *Frankenstein*, at Lord Byron's Swiss home while on holiday in 1818.

Brontosaurus was the heaviest of all dinosaurs. It weighed the same as five adult African elephants, which is about 30 tonnes.

Brontosaurus was a plant-eater and as it had a long neck, the creature could stretch up and eat the vegetation from the tops of the trees.

This dinosaur roamed around our planet over 140 million years ago and its remains have been discovered in North America.

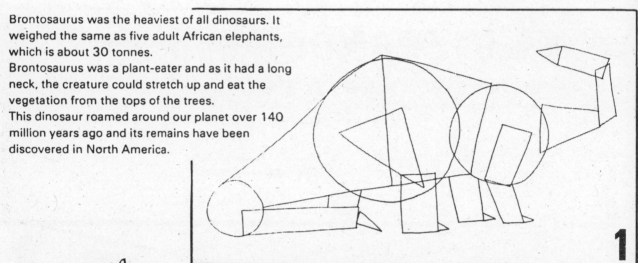

Let's draw a

BRONTOSAURUS

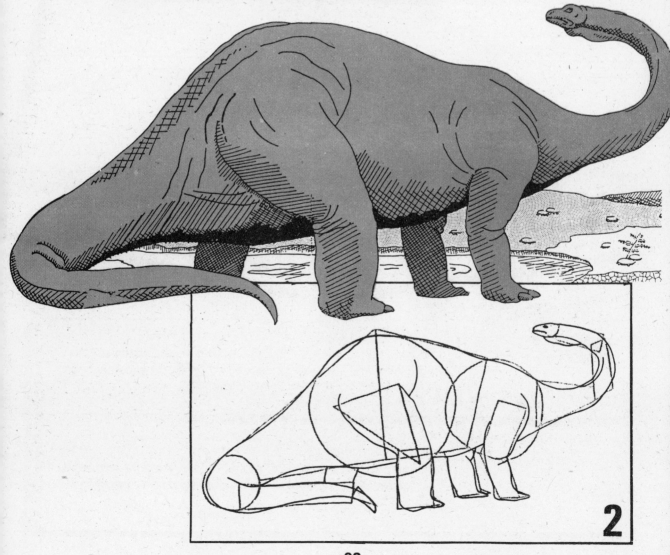

Let's draw a PTERANODON

Pteranodon was one of the largest flying reptiles. It measured about eight metres from the tip of one wing to the tip of the other wing. Unlike a bird it could not take off from the ground. To fly, it would launch itself, like a glider, off the edge of a cliff and spread its huge wings. The air currents that blew from the sea supported the Pteranodon and stopped it falling like a stone. It could then glide about while looking for food. To get food it would dive down into the sea and catch fish with its huge beak and then glide up again to the top of the cliff.

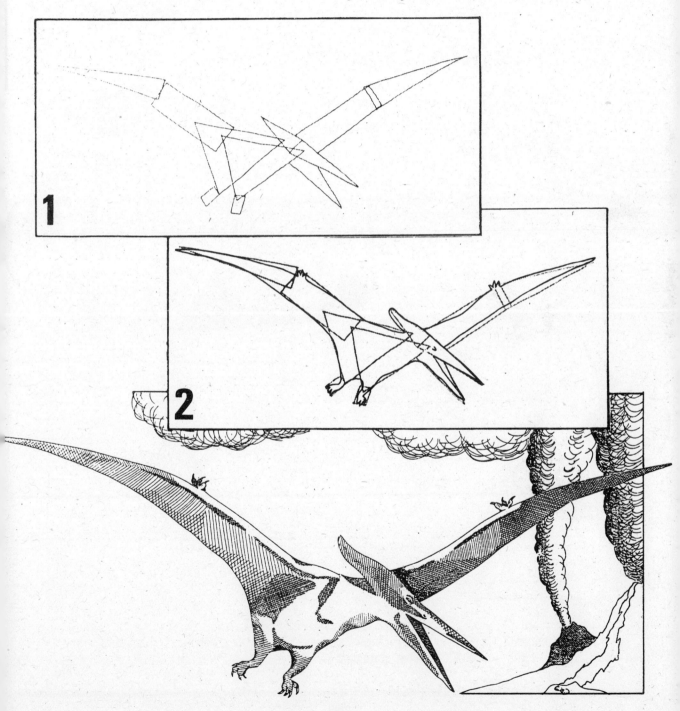

22

Cockneys are defined as Londoners born within the sound of Bow Church bells. In fact, the bells remained silent for twenty-two years between 1939 and 1961.

Twenty-two carat gold contains a minimum percentage of 91.66 of that metal.

All the rubber trees found today in south-east Asia are offspring of twenty-two plants grown in Sri Lanka just over 100 years ago.

THE POTATO GARDEN

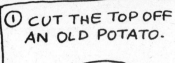

① CUT THE TOP OFF AN OLD POTATO.

② SLICE A PIECE OFF THE OTHER END SO THE POTATO WILL STAND UNSUPPORTED.

③ SCOOP A HOLE OUT OF THE TOP.

④ FILL THE HOLE WITH DAMP COTTON WOOL.

⑤ SPRINKLE SOME MUSTARD AND CRESS SEEDS ONTO THE COTTON WOOL.

SEEDS

⑥ KEEP THE POTATO IN A DARK PLACE UNTIL THE CRESS AND MUSTARD ARE ABOUT 25mm (1in) HIGH

I WAS A BIT DOUBTFUL AT FIRST, BUT THE IDEA JUST GREW ON ME!

Why didn't the shark eat the woman who fell off the ship?
Because it was a man-eating shark.

Knock, knock.
Who's there?
Alison.
Alison who?
Alison to what the teacher says but I never understand it.

The school-teacher was furious when Alec knocked him down with his new bicycle in the playground.
'Don't you know how to ride that yet?' he roared.
'Oh yes!' shouted Alec over his shoulder. 'It's the bell I can't work yet.'

Mother: 'The florist has two children.'
Alec: 'I know, one is a budding genius and the other is a blooming idiot!'

What happened to the burglar who fell in the concrete mixer?
He became a hardened criminal.

'What's the best cure for water on the brain?'
'A tap on the head!'

When the natural history teacher took Alec's class for a ramble, Alec tapped her on the shoulder and asked her what sort of animal has twenty legs, half of them blue, half of them green, sharp quills, three eyes and a huge nose.
'I've no idea, Alec,' she said. 'Why do you ask?'
'Because whatever it is, there's one crawling up your back.'

Why do bulldogs have flat faces?
From chasing parked cars.

Mother: 'Did you give the goldfish fresh water?'
Alec: 'No, they haven't drunk what I gave them yesterday.'

'I suppose this horrible picture is what you call modern art?'
'No, it's a mirror!'

Friend: 'My brother often has something on his mind.'
Alec: 'Only when he wears a hat.'

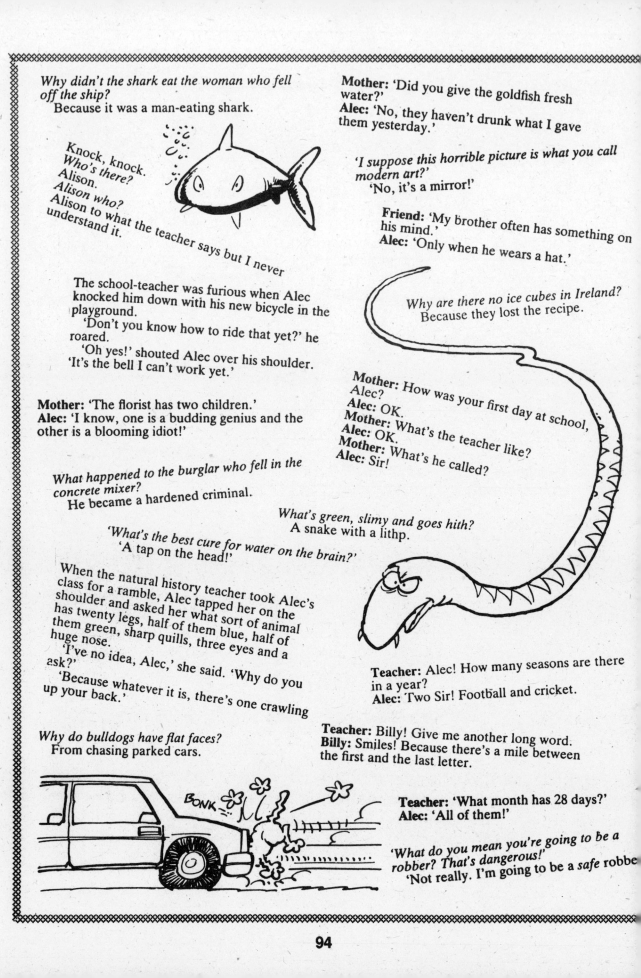

Why are there no ice cubes in Ireland?
Because they lost the recipe.

Mother: How was your first day at school, Alec?
Alec: OK.
Mother: What's the teacher like?
Alec: OK.
Mother: What's he called?
Alec: Sir!

What's green, slimy and goes hith?
A snake with a lithp.

Teacher: Alec! How many seasons are there in a year?
Alec: Two Sir! Football and cricket.

Teacher: Billy! Give me another long word.
Billy: Smiles! Because there's a mile between the first and the last letter.

BONK

Teacher: 'What month has 28 days?'
Alec: 'All of them!'

'What do you mean you're going to be a robber? That's dangerous!'
'Not really. I'm going to be a *safe* robbe

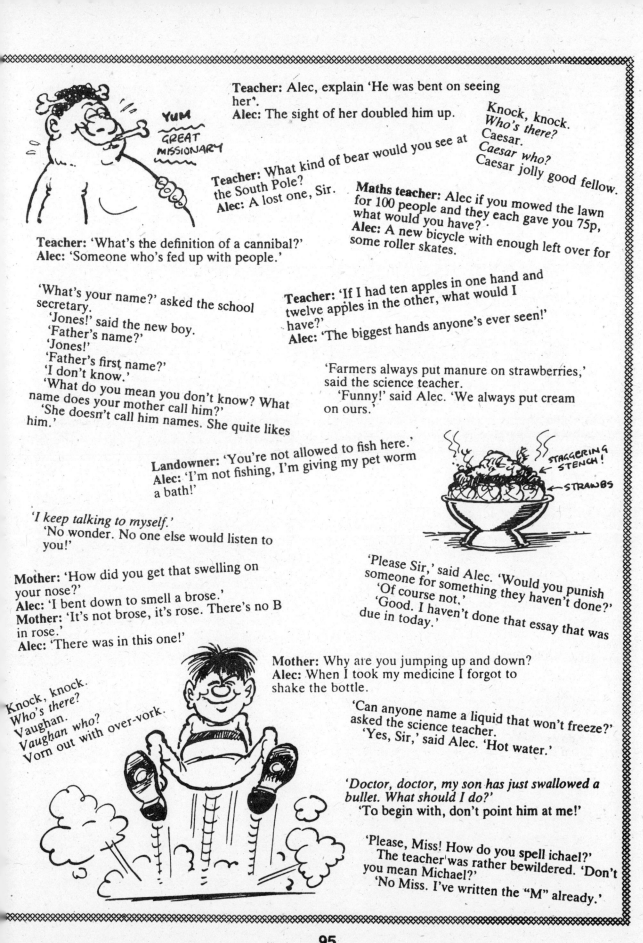

Teacher: Alec, explain 'He was bent on seeing her'.
Alec: The sight of her doubled him up.

Knock, knock.
Who's there?
Caesar.
Caesar who?
Caesar jolly good fellow.

Teacher: What kind of bear would you see at the South Pole?
Alec: A lost one, Sir.

Maths teacher: Alec if you mowed the lawn for 100 people and they each gave you 75p, what would you have?
Alec: A new bicycle with enough left over for some roller skates.

Teacher: 'What's the definition of a cannibal?'
Alec: 'Someone who's fed up with people.'

'What's your name?' asked the school secretary.
'Jones!' said the new boy.
'Father's name?'
'Jones!'
'Father's first name?'
'I don't know.'
'What do you mean you don't know? What name does your mother call him?'
'She doesn't call him names. She quite likes him.'

Teacher: 'If I had ten apples in one hand and twelve apples in the other, what would I have?'
Alec: 'The biggest hands anyone's ever seen!'

'Farmers always put manure on strawberries,' said the science teacher.
'Funny!' said Alec. 'We always put cream on ours.'

Landowner: 'You're not allowed to fish here.'
Alec: 'I'm not fishing, I'm giving my pet worm a bath!'

'I keep talking to myself.'
'No wonder. No one else would listen to you!'

Mother: 'How did you get that swelling on your nose?'
Alec: 'I bent down to smell a brose.'
Mother: 'It's not brose, it's rose. There's no B in rose.'
Alec: 'There was in this one!'

'Please Sir,' said Alec. 'Would you punish someone for something they haven't done?'
'Of course not.'
'Good. I haven't done that essay that was due in today.'

Mother: Why are you jumping up and down?
Alec: When I took my medicine I forgot to shake the bottle.

'Can anyone name a liquid that won't freeze?' asked the science teacher.
'Yes, Sir,' said Alec. 'Hot water.'

Knock, knock.
Who's there?
Vaughan.
Vaughan who?
Vorn out with over-vork.

'Doctor, doctor, my son has just swallowed a bullet. What should I do?'
'To begin with, don't point him at me!'

'Please, Miss! How do you spell ichael?'
The teacher was rather bewildered. 'Don't you mean Michael?'
'No Miss. I've written the "M" already.'

23

G.F.Handel (1685–1759) was fifty-six when he wrote his inspired oratorio *The Messiah*. He completed it in only twenty-three days, and during that time never left his room and often forgot his meals.

The Earth tilts at an angle of 23½°, which produces the seasonal changes.

Napoleon Bonaparte began to go bald when he was twenty-three.

GO BY WATER

NAVIGATION
NAVY

OARS
OCEAN

BOATS
BUOY

PASSAGE

CANOE
CRUISES

RIVER

DECKS

SAILING
SEAFARING
SHIPS

HELM

NAUTICAL

VOYAGE

YACHT

Clue: For which you need oars (6 letters)

24

There are twenty-four time zones, each equal to 15° latitude. The Soviet Union spans eleven of them.

There are twenty-four classifications of birds and twenty-four orders of insects.

By the age of twenty-four an Indian (Asian) elephant can respond to twenty-four words of command from its mahout.

WOHHCHA WIXYM

ABOVE IS A DEVIOUSLY CUNNING CODED MESSAGE WHICH MEANS 'CUNNING CODES'!

SECRET CODES ARE GREAT FUN — YOU CAN WRITE TO FRIENDS YOU SHARE THE CODE WITH AND NO ONE WILL BE ABLE TO UNDERSTAND WHAT YOU'RE WRITING ABOUT.

OR YOU CAN KEEP A DIARY IN CODE AND BE AS RUDE AS YOU LIKE, FOR IF ANYONE PICKS IT UP THEY WON'T BE ABLE TO MAKE HEAD OR TAIL OF IT.

HERE'S A VERY SIMPLE CODE. WRITE OUT THE LETTERS OF THE ALPHABET IN ONE LINE.

ABCDEFGHIJKLMNOPQRSTUVWXYZ

On the line below write out the letters of the alphabet again, but start the 'A' under any one of the other letters in the first line. For example:

A B C D E F G H I J K L M N O P Q R S T U V W X Y Z
U V W X Y Z A B C D E F G H I J K L M N O P Q R S T

'HIQ SIO BUPY U MYWLYN WIXY...'

We started the second alphabet under 'G', because we planned the code in July, which is the seventh month of the year, and 'G' is the seventh letter of the alphabet. On August 1, change the key to the code by moving the second line on by one letter, so that H=A, I=B and so on, and move them all along by one again on September 1.

clever, eh?

25

When the *QEII* sails to New York, clocks go back one hour every night for the five nights of the voyage, so passengers enjoy a twenty-five hour day and arrive fresh and free of the jet lag entailed in flying the Atlantic.

Most people blink about twenty-five times a minute.

A flowering plant contains at least twenty-five different types of cell.

Life or Death for Jerry

by Charles Bray

The tiny cockpit vibrated as Jerry Dawson slipped into top gear and slammed his foot on the throttle pedal. Responding sharply, the old racing car rocketed along Hangar Straight, and Jerry's eyes darted to his speedometer.

100 mph. . . 110 mph. . . 120 mph. . .

He set his eyes on two dots in the distance. Crash barriers, marshals and photographers were all lost in a blur as they seemed to flash by on either side of the car. The faster Jerry went, the larger the two dots became, until they were recognizable as two racing cars.

If I can pass them before the next corner, I'm in for a fast lap, thought Jerry.

The quicker Jerry went in practice, the further up the starting grid he would be for the afternoon race.

Within seconds he had caught the first car. It was Joe Harvey, an American, driving a March 773. The nose of Jerry's Chevron was only inches behind the rear of the March. Jerry suddenly flicked his steering wheel to the right, and pulled out of Harvey's slipstream. He passed him easily, but then winced when he saw who was in the other car.

"Oh, no, not Banzini," he moaned. "This is not going to be easy."

> Knock, knock.
> Who's there?
> Sally.
> Sally who?
> 'S-alligators I'm afraid of.
>
> What do geese watch on TV?
> Duckumentaries.
>
> Knock, knock.
> Who's there?
> Ivan.
> Ivan who?
> Ivan to hear you scream.

> What do Italian ghosts eat?
> Spookhetti.
>
> Algy met a bear.
> The bear met Algy.
> The bear grew bulgy.
> The bulge was Algy.
>
> Did the bionic monster have a brother?
> No, but he had a lot of trans-sisters.

Today was the big one for Jerry. He had battled against the might of the top Formula Three teams all season. He was only nineteen and ran his little racing team on a shoestring budget with no sponsorship, one old car and very few spares. Against all odds he had won four races and was currently second in the championship table, behind the experienced Italian, Mario Banzini.

If he could beat Banzini at Silverstone today, he would win the Formula Three title outright and stand a good chance of being signed up by a Formula One team. If he lost, he was out of racing – all his money had gone and he would probably have to sell up.

Jerry tucked the nose of his car right behind Banzini's red Ralt BMW. He could see into Banzini's mirrors and the Italian had a thunderous expression on his face. No way was he going to pass the reigning champion without a struggle. Stowe Corner loomed nearer and nearer.

"This is it!" yelled Jerry above the scream of his powerful engine.

He edged his car alongside Banzini and the two cars careered into the corner side by side. It was a battle of nerves and Jerry knew that the last one to brake would be the first one out of the corner. It seemed for a moment that neither car would give in as the corner loomed dangerously close. The rear tyres of each car touched, sending up a puff of blue smoke. Jerry's heart pounded and his knuckles turned white as he gripped the tiny steering wheel with all his might. They were almost into the corner now.

Banzini suddenly braked and sparks flew as his nose cone dipped and scraped against the rough tarmac.

Jerry braked a split second later – almost too late. His car screamed into the corner in front of the Italian. All four

Knock, knock.
Who's there?
Annie.
Annie who?
Annie body here
seen Kelly.

I can't stop telling
lies.
I don't believe you.

The way he moans and groans when he gets even the slightest cold, you can't decide whether to call a doctor or a drama critic!

wheels locked up under the violent braking and clouds of blue smoke rose from the tyres as the rubber began to burn. The car slid straight towards the crash barrier at tremendous speed and Jerry screwed up his face in horror.

Just in time, the back end of the car spun round and the rear wheel bounced off the metal crash barrier. The Chevron began a vicious slide across the circuit, right in front of Banzini. Miraculously the two cars missed each other and Jerry fought furiously to control his wayward car. He slammed his foot on the accelerator and powered out of the slide, still in front of the Italian.

He glanced at his mirrors and could see Banzini right behind him, angrily shaking his fist.

And this was just the practice session! It should be one heck of a race.

Jerry had lost a bit of time at the last corner. If this was still going to be his fast lap, he would have to take the next corner perfectly.

But Jerry never made it to the next corner.

The Italian was driving furiously. The nose of the Ralt BMW edged closer and closer to Jerry. Suddenly it rammed one of Jerry's rear wheels. The tyre exploded and bits of black rubber flew into the air amidst a cloud of smoke. The car veered crazily to its left and slid sideways into the crash barrier at tremendous speed.

Marshals and ambulance men ran across to the wrecked Chevron, and Banzini disappeared around Club Corner. Amazingly, Jerry climbed out unhurt, and began his long walk back to the pits.

By the time Jerry reached the pits his wrecked car had arrived. It hung pathetically from the back of a large breakdown wagon. The mechanics lowered it gently to the ground. Jerry had just started to examine it when his brother Peter walked up. Peter was three years older than Jerry and acted as his pit mechanic.

"If we ever get it fixed, I'll stick a set of 'L' plates on it," he joked.

Jerry spun around angrily. "That Italian is a madman!" he shouted. "He nearly killed me. We'll never make the race now."

"It's tough at the top," laughed Peter, risking a punch on the nose. "We'll have to fix it somehow, little brother, or we'll be out of work next year."

However, even Peter's optimism faded as he carefully examined the damage. The nose cone was completely crumpled and the suspension bars on both nearside wheels were badly buckled. A rear wheel was totally wrecked and the side body panel was hanging down in two pieces.

The two brothers were staring glumly at the damage when Mario Banzini walked up. He stood glowering in his smart red driving suit, his swarthy face and black moustache making him look even angrier.

A traveller from Lake Tana
Took a trip to Ghana.
He brought a packed lunch
To quietly munch,
Of three dates and one ripe banana.

Friend: I think Josephine has a big mouth.
Alec: Put it this way. She eats bananas sideways!

Alec: You need glasses.
Father: Why do you say that?
Alec: There's newsprint on the tip of your nose!

What does a ghost keep in its cellar?
Whines and spirits.

Knock, knock.
Who's there?
Benny.
Benny who?
Benny for your thoughts.

"Little boys should not compete with men," he leered, in broken English. "This is no sport for babies. You must learn to drive properly and try again in a few years."

The Italian turned on his heels and left the pits before Jerry or his brother could answer. Jerry watched Banzini climb into a brand new racing transporter. It was bright red and emblazoned on the side in huge gold letters were the words: MARIO BANZINI – RACING FOR ITALY.

Jerry looked at his own battered Transit van and rusty old trailer. He turned angrily to his brother and snarled, "Peter, we're going to race this afternoon – even if it kills us."

The two brothers worked like slaves throughout the rest of the morning. They carefully knocked out most of the dints on the nose cone and painstakingly straightened the suspension bars. Peter welded the two pieces of body panel together and Jerry managed to swap his only set of spare racing tyres for a new rear wheel.

Slowly and carefully they reassembled the car. They finished fifteen minutes before the start of the race. The Chevron still looked a sorry sight, but at least it was raceworthy.

> Knock, knock.
> Who's there?
> Leon.
> Leon who?
> Leigh-on-Sea is near Southend.
>
> Alec: I have almost 3000 bones in my body.
> Teacher: You know that's not possible.
> Alec: Yes it is. I had a can of sardines for lunch!

Jerry was delighted, and he grew happier still when he heard that his practice time had put him on the third row of the starting grid. He pulled on his helmet, climbed into the Chevron and drove on to the starting grid.

The battered Chevron looked out of place among the other gleaming Formula Three cars. The minutes ticked away and the pit marshals eventually cleared the track of the hundreds of mechanics, photographers and hangers on.

Banzini was sitting on the front row. He turned around in his seat and studied the patched-up Chevron. His face broke into an evil smile.

Jerry looked away. Tension was mounting and he needed every ounce of concentration.

The starter appeared and held up the 'thirty seconds to go' board. Thirty highly tuned racing engines rasped into life and the noise was deafening as the Union Jack was raised.

The flag dropped and the cars roared off towards Coppice Corner like a swarm of angry bees. Banzini was first into the corner and already drawing away from the rest of the pack. Jerry lost valuable time in the opening yards with rear wheel spin and was in eighth position as the

> Where do cows go for entertainment? To the mooovies.
>
> Knock, knock.
> Who's there?
> Ronnie.
> Ronnie who?
> Ronnie butter spreads more quickly.
>
> Do you think he has many faults? Only two: what he says and what he does!

105

tightly bunched cars left the first corner and headed out towards Maggots Curve.

Racing as if his life depended on it, Jerry began to pick off the other cars. With ten laps to go he was in third place. The Chevron roared along Hangar Straight at 130 mph and

Knock, knock.
Who's there?
Tom.
Tom who?
Tom A Tosoup.

I'm teacher's pet, said Alec when he came home from school.
That's nice dear, said Mum. How do you know?
'Cos he puts kisses by all my sums.

then dropped down quickly through the gears as it approached Stowe Corner. Jerry saw the second placed car, a blue March, approach the bend on a wide line. He swept round on the inside of it at 80 mph. Before the March driver knew what was happening, Jerry had shot past him and was accelerating away from the bend.

Only one man to catch now – Banzini!

He set off after the Italian like a rocket. The large crowd was on its feet as the two cars flashed past the main grandstands only two seconds apart. The tatty Chevron drew closer and closer to the bright red Ralt BMW . . . but Banzini had no intention of being overtaken.

He began to weave erratically across the track, shutting out Jerry each time he tried to edge past him. Jerry had to brake hard and sit it out behind the Italian as they both hurtled towards the corner. Banzini kept up these tactics for the next four laps and as Jerry began his last lap, his hopes of winning faded.

Only inches separated the two cars as they approached Club Corner for the last time. Jerry thought quickly. He would try to fool Banzini here. He set up his car for the bend as if to try for the outside of the Ralt BMW. As expected, the Italian moved over to his left to shut him out. Like lightning, Jerry shot through on the inside and the two cars left the bend side by side, the rear wheels of Jerry's car level with the front wheels of Banzini's. Jerry felt a terrific thump on his rear tyre, followed by three or four lighter thumps. The rear of his car bounced about violently as the Ralt BMW was continually driven into him.

Amazingly, his tyre stayed intact and he managed to pull in front of the crazy Italian.

Half a lap to go!

Try as he might, Jerry could not pull away from the red car. Banzini stayed in Jerry's slipstream, inches behind him. He tried every dirty trick in the book to regain his lead. Time after time he rammed his nose cone into the rear of the Chevron, each time missing the rear tyres and colliding with the gear box. Jerry held his breath as a piece of exhaust pipe broke away from his car and flew into the air.

The engine sounded really rough now, rather like an old tractor, but still he clung on to his narrow lead.

As they accelerated out of Woodcote Corner, Banzini drew level with Jerry and the two cars hurtled side by side towards the chequered flag. Oil gushed from the Chevron's battered gearbox and an ugly plume of smoke rose from the back of the car.

Most of the oil was blown on to the smooth rear tyres of the red Ralt BMW. Suddenly, the tyres lost their adhesion and Banzini went into a violent, uncontrollable spin. He slid off the circuit into the crash barrier.

Jerry flashed past the chequered flag, to the delight of the hysterical crowd. He waved frantically to his brother in the pits, and began his slowing down lap.

How do you make a
skeleton laugh?
Tickle his funny
bone.

Above the roar of the crowd and the scream of his tired engine, he could just hear the announcer's voice.

"What a win by young Jerry Dawson! We're sure to see him in Formula One next season."

26

Fortnum and Mason's, the renowned Piccadilly store, in business since 1707, sells twenty-six kinds of mustard.

A single sheep's fleece might well contain as many as twenty-six million fibres.

Twenty-six weddings take place at St Paul's Cathedral, London, each year. The most notable of recent times was that of the Prince and Princess of Wales in 1981.

27

The Duke of Wellington's charger, Copenhagen, died in 1835, twenty years after Waterloo, aged twenty-seven.

Each human hand contains twenty-seven small bones.

A xylophone is a musical instrument consisting of twenty-seven bars of specially prepared wood arranged in rows over resonators. The notes are produced by striking the bars with two small hammers, one held in each hand.

The Valley

Take the bird to the nest.

Begin *

* End

110

CAR GAMES

PUB TENNIS

PLAYERS DIVIDE INTO TWO TEAMS. ONE TEAM TAKES THE RIGHT SIDE OF THE ROAD, AND THE OTHER THE LEFT. THE FIRST PLAYER TO SEE A PUB ON HIS TEAM'S SIDE CALLS OUT '15-LOVE'. IF A PLAYER ON THE OTHER TEAM SPOTS A PUB ON HIS SIDE NEXT HE CALLS OUT '15-ALL'. IF NOT, WHEN THE FIRST TEAM SPOT THEIR SECOND PUB, THEY CALL OUT '30-LOVE'.

IF THE SCORE GETS TO 40-40 ('DEUCE') A TEAM HAS TO WIN BY TWO CLEAR POINTS. IF THEY GET ONE, THEY HAVE 'ADVANTAGE'; AND THEY WIN THE GAME IF THEY SEE ANOTHER PUB BEFORE THE OTHER TEAM.

FIRST TO REACH SIX GAMES WINS THE SET.

GOING TO GLASGOW

One of the passengers calls out a place name, and another player must say he's going there; how he intends to travel and what he's going to do when he gets there — all starting with the initial letter of the place name.

So if someone calls 'Glasgow', you would say, 'I'm Going to Glasgow by Galloping to Gather Grapefruit'.

Poor Sid's not quite sure how he's going to get to Zanzibar! ('by ZEPPELIN TO ZIP ZITHERS' maybe?)

Arabic consists of twenty-eight letters, all of them consonants, with vowels indicated by small marks either above or below. It is written from right to left.

The world's loftiest peak – Mount Everest (8,848 m; 29,028 ft) – is situated in Nepal, almost exactly on the line of latitude 28° North.

Centipedes have between 28 and 354 legs.

SOUP

ASPARAGUS

BARLEY
BISK
BLACK BEAN
BORSCHT
BOUILLON

GUMBO

LEEK

MINESTRONE
MUSHROOM

OKRA
ONION
OXTAIL
OYSTER

VEGETABLE

A	N	M	O	O	R	H	S	U	M
S	A	G	U	M	B	O	Y	B	I
P	E	T	O	I	N	E	O	O	N
A	B	M	S	I	L	R	R	X	E
R	K	K	O	R	S	E	L	T	S
A	C	N	A	C	T	E	A	A	T
G	A	B	H	S	E	A	R	I	R
U	L	T	Y	K	T	O	K	L	O
S	B	O	U	I	L	L	O	N	N
V	E	G	E	T	A	B	L	E	E

Clue: Reddish coloured soup (6 letters)

A Gaelic harp has twenty-nine brass strings. They are plucked by the fingers, the nails of which are grown long for the purpose.

Only 29 per cent of the world's surface is covered by land.

With a maximum speed of 29 mph (46 kph), George Stephenson's railway engine *Rocket* won the Rainham trials in 1829, and earned for its designer a prize of £500.

Limerick Fun

A very strange thing is a newt –
It seldom, if ever, eats fruit.
It dwells in ponds
Living on fronds
And says not a word – it's mute.

There was a young man called Paul
Who decided to paper the hall.
From ceiling to ground
He papered around –
Now you can't see the doors at all!

The composer Benjamin Britten,
Owned a musical kitten.
It played lovely tunes
On piano and spoons,
Much better than Britten had written.

A swimmer in the Adriatic
Was floating about quite static.
But when he saw
A fin and a jaw,
His movements became quite dramatic!

Daily life is confusing
And really not very amusing.
Machines are robotic;
The traffic's chaotic;
So I simply avoid it by snoozing.

At Christmas we visit Aunt Molly
Who's usually funny and jolly;
But last Boxing day,
Her temper gave way
When she fell in a load of green holly.

I knew a girl named Monica;
She lives in Greece, in Salonika.
In the dark of the night
With the stars shining bright,
She skilfully plays the harmonica.

ODD ONE OUT

Which is the odd one out in each group?

COUNTRY FOOD

Can you pair up each type of food with its country of origin.

A. HAGGIS
B. SPAGHETTI
C. HOT DOGS
D. GOULASH
E. CURRY

1. ITALY
2. HUNGARY
3. INDIA
4. SCOTLAND
5. AMERICA

GIRLS NAMES

The first letter of each picture will spell their names.

NAME THE COUNTRIES

FIND THE NAMES FROM THE PICTURE CLUES

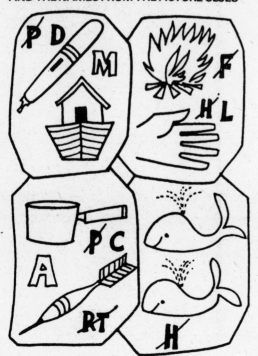

the EXPLORER

HUGO FIRST, THE FAMOUS EXPLORER, HAS FOUND A SECRET MESSAGE. CAN YOU DE-CODE IT, USING THE KEY?

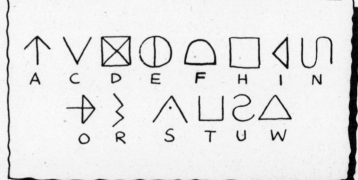

A C D E F H I N

O R S T U W

FIND THE BIRD!

Re-arrange the letters to find the names of the birds.

KLAR

WNAS

OCUCOK

EMAIPG

LKEESRT

NRIOB

NBRA LOW

SPOT THE DIFFERENCES
These two illustrations appear to be exactly alike, but there are five things missing in the one on the right. Can you find them?

WHAT IS HIDDEN HERE?
What is hidden behind all these squares? If you fill in all the squares with the black dots, a drawing will suddenly appear.

MYSTERY MEN
Only one of these silhouettes is exactly the same as the one at the top left of the drawing. Which one is it?

30

It is possible to accommodate thirty people at a time inside the gigantic head of the Statue of Liberty, which stands on Bedloe's island in New York harbour.

For thirty days during Ramadan, a true Moslem will not touch food from dawn until sunset. He is allowed only heavily sugared tea.

After the age of thirty people begin to shrink!

HOW OLD IS YOUR GRANNY?

IF YOU WANT TO FIND OUT HOW OLD YOUR GRANNY IS, BUT SHE WON'T TELL YOU, TRICK HER INTO GIVING HER AGE AWAY...

ASK HER TO THINK OF THE MONTH SHE WAS BORN (JANUARY = 1, FEBRUARY = 2, MARCH = 3, AND SO ON), BUT NOT TO TELL YOU. SUPPOSE SHE WAS BORN IN MARCH 1920 : SHE'D BE 67. THIS IS HOW YOU WORK IT OUT:

ASK YOUR GRANNY TO:

a) DOUBLE THE MONTH $3 \times 2 = 6$
b) ADD FIVE TO THE TOTAL $6 + 5 = 11$
c) MULTIPLY BY 50 $11 \times 50 = 550$
d) NOW ADD ON HER AGE $550 + 67 = 617$
e) SUBTRACT 250 $617 - 250 = 367$

AND TELL YOU THE ANSWER : 367

GRANNY, YOU WERE BORN IN MARCH, AND YOU WERE 67 LAST BIRTHDAY.

THE FIRST DIGIT IS THE MONTH (3 = MARCH) AND THE LAST TWO HER AGE! IF THE ANSWER SHE GIVES YOU HAS **FOUR** DIGITS, THE FIRST TWO WILL BE THE MONTH (10 = OCTOBER, 11 = NOVEMBER, etc) AND THE LAST TWO WILL BE HER AGE.

clever, eh?

117

FINISH THE SAYINGS

| AS WISE AS AN |
| AS THIN AS A |
| AS CLEAR AS A |
| AS FIT AS A |
| AS SLIPPERY AS AN |

SIX DIFFERENCES

There are 6 differences between the two pictures. How quickly can you find them?

Limerick Fun

I feel a chilly breeze;
It's colder by degrees.
My throat is sore,
And what is more,
I think I have to sneeze.

There was a young boy called Jim
Who fractured his right lower limb.
He leapt in a pool
Without water – the fool.
Good heavens, he must have been dim!

There was a young man called Dale
Who wanted to eat a whale.
He mashed it with cheese,
And served it with peas,
But couldn't quite manage the tail.

There was a young lady of Twickenham,
Whose boots were too small to walk quickenham.
She bore them awhile;
But at last, at a stile,
She took them both off and was sickenham.

A man from the Appalachians
Breeds the best dalmatians.
He knows that their spots
Appeal to lots
Of people from all generations.

There was a young man from Australia
Who tried to grow an azalea.
He nearly went crazy
When up popped a daisy –
What a horticultural failure.

There was an old man from Dunoon
Who set out on a trip by balloon.
The man came off worst
When the big balloon burst,
And he landed back home rather soon.

31

In order to send Lord Nelson's inspired battle call, 'England expects that every man will do his duty', to the other twenty-six ships of the fleet at Trafalgar in 1805, the signaller of the *Victory* had to hoist thirty-one flags.

Thirty-one years are equivalent to a billion seconds.

There are thirty-one Beefeaters, or more correctly, Yeoman Warders, at the Tower of London.

Place the Words

FIT THE PICTURE NAMES INTO THE SQUARES ACROSS, TO FIND ANOTHER WORD IN THE SQUARES GOING DOWN.

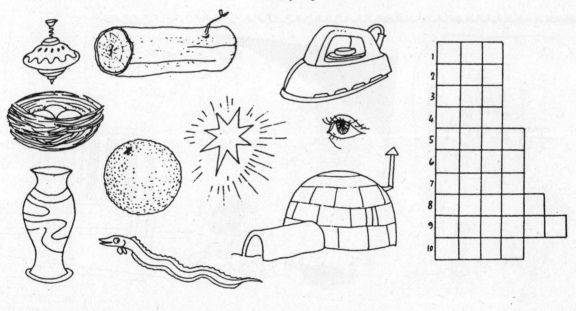

COIN PUZZLE

Place nine coins or buttons on the table as shown in the drawing. The coins are numbered to explain the solution.

The rule of the game is to move three—only three—of the coins, so that the triangle points upwards.

OUT OF ORDER

T	P	Y	S	M	P	S	E	E	D
L	O	S	A	U	U	L	S	I	L
M	E	P	L	R	B	D	S	U	R
M	I	U	S	M	R	H	D	A	M
E	O	S	A	Y	A	A	M	L	H
F	L	R	H	R	T	P	S	A	E
T	C	B	M	M	A	U	S	I	S
S	O	O	M	G	A	S	R	T	D
M	N	I	E	U	L	S	I	V	E
Y	L	S	R	E	J	R	H	L	Y

DISHARMONY
DISARRAY

FOUL-UP

HASSLE

JUMBLE

MESS
MISH-MASH
MUDDLE
MUSS

RAMPAGES
RIOT

SCRAMBLE
STIR

TOPSY-TURVY

Clue: In disarray (4,4 letters)

GARDENING with DAFFY DILL

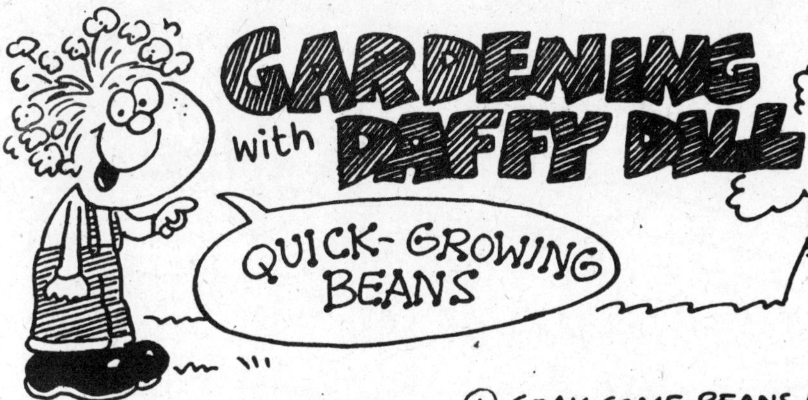

QUICK-GROWING BEANS

Sid wants to know what's a cannibal's favourite snack? HUMAN BEANS ON TOAST!

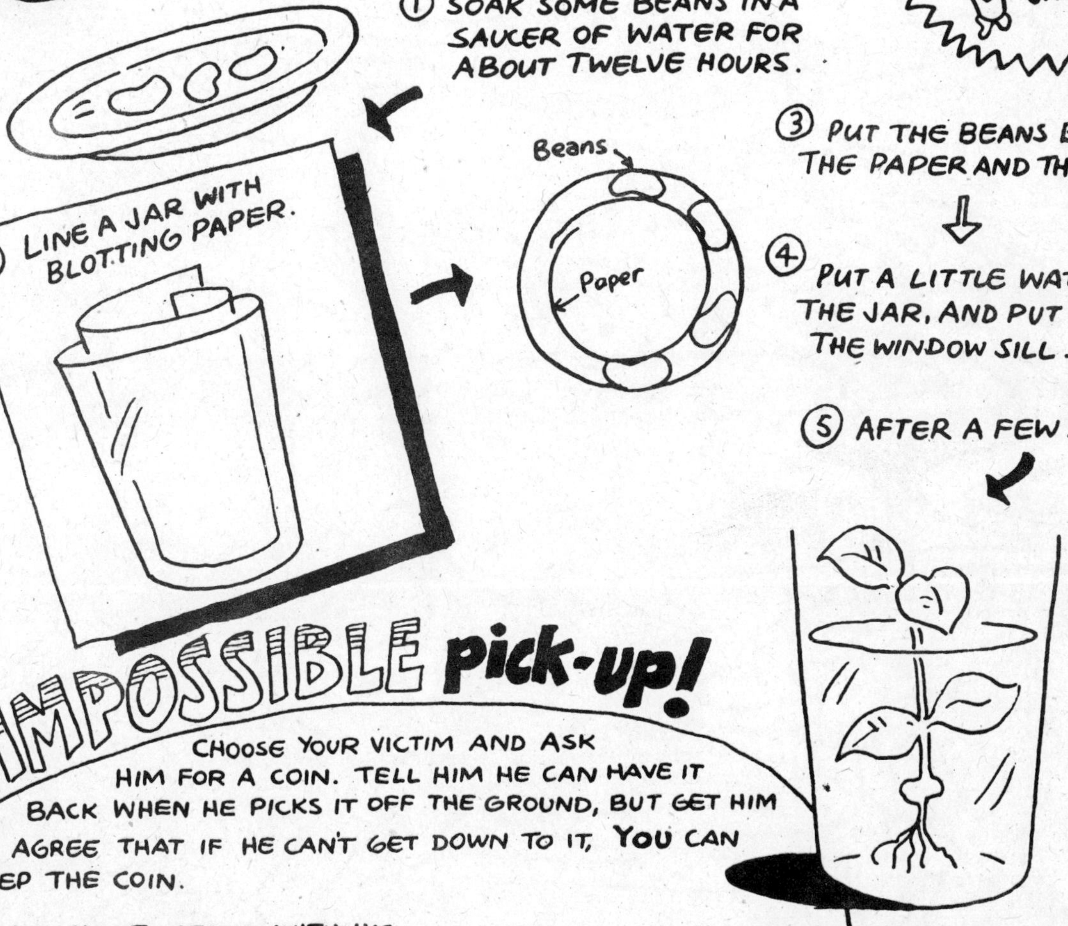

① SOAK SOME BEANS IN A SAUCER OF WATER FOR ABOUT TWELVE HOURS.

② LINE A JAR WITH BLOTTING PAPER.

Beans

Paper

③ PUT THE BEANS BETWEEN THE PAPER AND THE GLASS.

④ PUT A LITTLE WATER IN THE JAR, AND PUT IT ON THE WINDOW SILL.

⑤ AFTER A FEW DAYS...

the IMPOSSIBLE pick-up!

CHOOSE YOUR VICTIM AND ASK HIM FOR A COIN. TELL HIM HE CAN HAVE IT BACK WHEN HE PICKS IT OFF THE GROUND, BUT GET HIM TO AGREE THAT IF HE CAN'T GET DOWN TO IT, YOU CAN KEEP THE COIN.

NOW ASK HIM TO STAND WITH HIS BACK AND HIS HEELS AGAINST A WALL ... PUT THE COIN 60cm (2ft) IN FRONT OF HIM AND TELL HIM TO PICK IT UP WITHOUT MOVING HIS HEELS FROM THE WALL, OR RAISING THEM OFF THE GROUND...,

...YOU'LL WIN THE COIN!!

WHEN THEY'RE ABOUT 10cm (4in) HIGH, YOU CAN PLANT THEM IN THE GARDEN.

Search

End

Begin

Help the girl to find her lost
handkerchief in the long grass.

122

32

A London Transport double-decker bus can lean an incredible 32° from upright without keeling over.

A gale is a wind that blows at 32 mph (51 kph) or more.

The ninth US President, William Henry Harrison (1773–1841), held office for only thirty-two days: 4 March to 5 April, 1841. He died of pneumonia, contracted at his inauguration when he inadvisedly spurned a hat and overcoat in cold and drizzly weather.

INDOOR FISHING

Cut fish shapes out of old newspaper and slip paper-clips over the ends. Scatter them over the bannister if you have one, or else on the floor.
Give anglers fishing rods made out of bits of garden canes and string, with a magnet tied at the end. Whoever hooks the most fish wins. It's an attractive way to angle.

I KNEW THE HOUSE WAS DAMP, BUT THIS IS RIDICULOUS!

33

Between the coldest and the hottest day, Sydney Harbour Bridge can 'grow' 33 cm (13 in) in length due to metal expansion.

A seemingly dry slice of bread in fact contains 33 per cent water.

The world's longest tunnel is the 33 mile (53 km) Seikan, which links the Japanese islands of Honshu and Hokkaido under the notoriously treacherous waters of the Tsuganu Strait.

Limerick Fun

A girl in Alice Springs
Had some water wings.
But in a drought,
There is no doubt
They're pretty hopeless things.

There was a dog, a Great Dane,
Who hadn't got much of a brain.
He'd chase a hare,
That just wasn't there,
And he'd do it again and again.

Thirty days have September,
April, June and November.
Most of the others have thirty-one:
An extra day to have some fun!

Little Miss Muffet
Sat on her tuffet
Eating chicken and chips:
Her sister who's hateful,
Ate half the plateful,
Then strolled away licking her lips.

A beautiful bird is the jay
With plumage exceedingly gay.
It chunters and chatters
On various matters,
Whilst flying along on its way.

There was a young fellow named Vivian
Who had a dear friend, a Bolivian,
Who dropped his cigar
In a gunpowder jar,
And blew himself into oblivion.

There was an old dame of Dunbar,
Who took the 4.4 to Forfar,
But it went on to Dundee,
So she travelled, you see,
Too far by 4.4 from Forfar.

A SHIP'S LANTERNS

Which colour are the lanterns on a ship's starboard side (the right-hand side): Red, Blue, Green or Yellow?

Bottle fiasco

The expression "a fiasco" which means that something didn't turn out right, has an unusual origin. "Fiasco" is actually an Italian word and means a bottle. When Italian glass blowers discovered a fault in the raw glass on which they were working, instead of throwing it away, they made a bottle out of the mass. And this is the origin of "fiasco".

THE EGGBOX GAME

Cut the top off an old eggbox and number each compartment with a felt-tip pen like this.

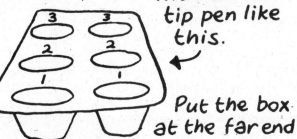

Put the box at the far end of a table and try to throw dried peas into the compartments, scoring as you go.

Each player is given six peas— so the maximum score is eighteen. Whoever scores most wins. The pea must stay in the compartment; if it bounces out, there's no score.

MEMORY TEST

LOOK AT THIS PAGE FOR ONE MINUTE, CLOSE THE BOOK AND SEE HOW MANY OBJECTS YOU REMEMBER.

Then there was the farmer who rolled his field because he wanted to grow mashed potatoes...

NURSERY RHYME CROSSWORD

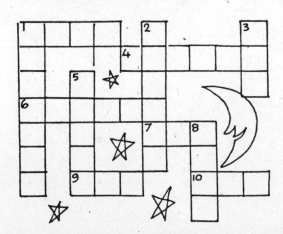

CLUES ACROSS:-
1. HOT CROSS _ _ _ _
4. HE HAD A GREAT FALL — SURNAME
6. SHE LOST HER SHEEP
7. THE PIPER'S SON
9. 'I HAD A LITTLE _ _ _ TREE'
10. A WISE OLD BIRD

CLUES DOWN
1. LITTLE _ _ _ _ _ _ _ COME BLOW YOUR HORN
2. CHRISTIAN NAME OF 4 ACROSS
3. ROCK-A-_ _ _ _ BABY
5. THE DISH RAN AWAY WITH THIS
8. THE COW JUMPED OVER THIS

It took Sir Francis Drake thirty-four months (December 1577 to September 1580) to sail round the world in the *Golden Hind*.

When the Indonesian island of Krakatoa erupted on 27 August 1883, it threw rocks 34 miles (54.7 km) high and destroyed 163 villages.

English is the first language of at least thirty-four countries, and is spoken by over 400 million people.

make a Ball and Cup Game

YOU'LL NEED:

- A BALL OF COTTON WOOL
- A CARDBOARD TUBE FROM THE INSIDE OF A TOILET ROLL
- ALUMINIUM FOIL
- GLUE
- A SHARP PENCIL
- STRING

① Cover the cardboard tube with the foil and fold the jagged edges down inside the tube. You don't have to glue the foil to the tube but if you do it will last longer.

② Pierce a hole with a sharp pencil through the cardboard close to one end.

③ Thread the string through the hole and knot it.

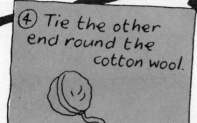

④ Tie the other end round the cotton wool.

⑤ Cover it with foil.

Have competitions with your friends to see who can catch the ball in the tube the most times.

Let's draw HIGH-SPEED TRAINS

High-speed Trains are often just called H.S.T. They are very fast diesel trains which set the diesel speed record of 230 k.p.h. in 1973. However, in service for British Rail their top speed is 200 k.p.h. They were first used by British Rail in the Western Region in 1974 and are now in use in the Eastern Region as well.

High-speed Trains are built to be as streamlined and light as possible. The coaches are 22 metres long and very comfortable. This is to keep the passengers happy. The driver also has a warm, comfortable cabin. There are lots of controls and warning lights and he has a large, unbreakable windscreen to look through.

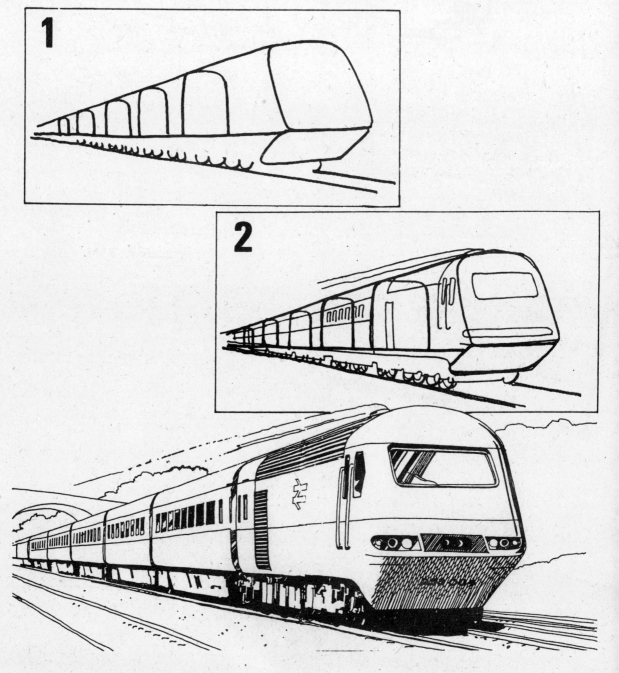

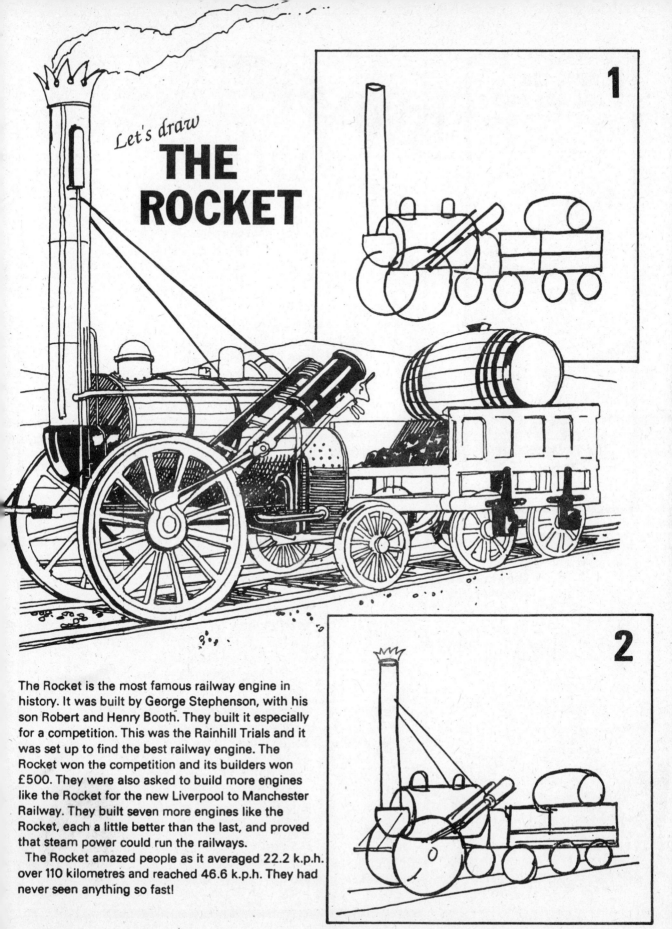

Let's draw
THE ROCKET

1

2

The Rocket is the most famous railway engine in history. It was built by George Stephenson, with his son Robert and Henry Booth. They built it especially for a competition. This was the Rainhill Trials and it was set up to find the best railway engine. The Rocket won the competition and its builders won £500. They were also asked to build more engines like the Rocket for the new Liverpool to Manchester Railway. They built seven more engines like the Rocket, each a little better than the last, and proved that steam power could run the railways.

The Rocket amazed people as it averaged 22.2 k.p.h. over 110 kilometres and reached 46.6 k.p.h. They had never seen anything so fast!

Spot the odd one out!

1
2
3
4
5
6
7
8
9

ZOO SIGNS

Help Tony the Tiger rearrange the jumbled letters to find his friends.

FIRE GAF

ECLC DIOR

ONK YNEM

HANE PTEL

BREAZ

ONL

MCALE

?

Limerick Fun

A dog I used to own,
Would never touch a bone.
He'd only eat
The finest meat,
And he'd order it by phone!

I eat peas with honey,
I've done it all my life.
They do taste kind of funny –
But it keeps them on the knife!

A lady who disliked the rhumba
Wanted to hear a new number.
She said, 'Please play
Something quite gay,
But quietly so I may slumber.'

There was a young man of Japan
Who wrote verse that never would scan.
When they said 'But the thing
Doesn't go with a swing,'
He said 'Yes but I always like to get as many words into the
    last line as I possibly can!'

There was a young man in Wales
Who didn't care much for the dales.
He got his thrills
From the highest hills,
Until blown away by strong gales.

There was a young man of Gloucester,
Who had a sweet girl, but then lost 'er.
Down a small country lane,
He found her again,
In a hedge where a bull had tossed 'er!

One day a poor nervous goose
Was frightened to death by a moose:
It stood on one leg
And laid a big egg;
Then all of its feathers came loose.

35

Walt Disney, inventor of the animated cartoon, won a record thirty-five Oscars between 1931 and 1969.

The standard 18 cm (7 in) pencil contains sufficient graphite to draw a line 35 miles (56 km) in length.

The 4.5 m (15 ft) long king cobra stores enough venom to kill thirty-five men or a fully-grown Indian elephant.

ABOUT BOATS

ALCORT

BOOM

DINGHY

FIBRE GLASS

GRUMMAN

HULL

INBOARD

JETS

KEEL

LAKE

LASER

MARINA

PADDLE

PONTOONS

RACING

SAILBOAT

SEAS

YACHTS

S	S	E	A	L	C	O	R	T	S
N	N	D	L	H	E	K	I	S	I
O	A	S	I	D	U	E	A	E	N
O	M	S	A	N	D	L	K	P	B
T	M	M	A	I	G	A	L	A	O
N	U	O	P	E	L	H	P	N	A
O	R	O	R	A	S	B	Y	I	R
P	G	B	S	T	E	J	O	R	D
E	I	E	R	G	N	I	C	A	R
F	R	Y	A	C	H	T	S	M	T

Clue: Boss of the boat (7 letters)

Slippery Sam's escape...

I was locked in a prison cell with only a wooden chair. How did I get out? HEH! HEH!

First I rubbed my hands together 'till they were sore; then I took the saw...

... and sawed the chair in half.

Two halves make a whole,

...then I shouted 'till I was hoarse.

so I crawled through the hole...

All I had to do then, was jump on the horse and off I galloped!

132

GIVING YOUR WORD

(A) BOTTICELLI

One player- 'Botticelli'- thinks of a character who may be alive or dead, fact or fiction. The others have to guess who he or she is by asking him such questions as, 'Are you a famous entertainer?' or 'Did you live in the eighteenth century?' They must be questions to which the answer will be either 'Yes' or 'No'.

If the answer is 'No', the questioning passes to the next player. If, however, the answer is 'Yes', whoever asked the question can either ask another question, or take a stab at guessing Botticelli's identity.

If, after ten direct attempts at guessing who Botticelli is, no one has solved the mystery, Botticelli confesses — and gets another go.

If a player does guess correctly, he takes over as Botticelli for the next round.

guess who?

(B) PORTMANTEAU

THE FIRST PLAYER STARTS, 'I PACKED MY BAG AND IN IT I PUT A VACUUM FLASK' (OR WHATEVER). THE NEXT PLAYER CONTINUES, 'I PACKED MY BAG AND IN IT I PUT A VACUUM FLASK AND A PAIR OF TRAINERS'. CONTINUE ROUND THE CIRCLE, EVERYONE REPEATING WHAT HAS ALREADY BEEN PACKED BEFORE ADDING THEIR OWN ITEMS... IF ANYONE MAKES A MISTAKE OR HESITATES FOR TOO LONG, THEY DROP OUT.

good game!

CHEEKY CHALLENGES

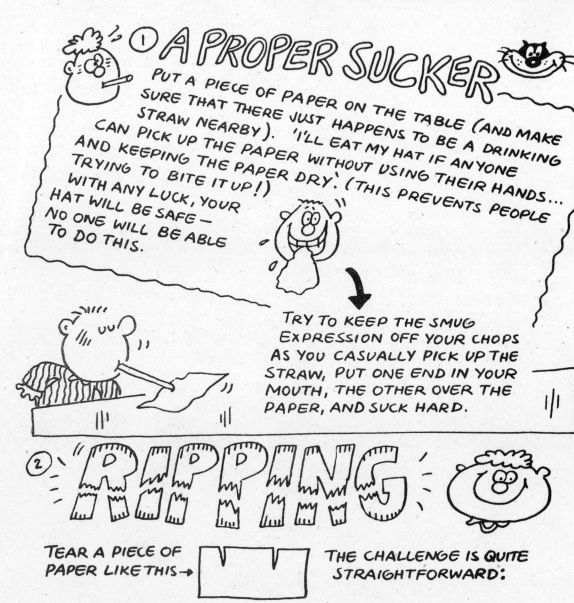

① A PROPER SUCKER

PUT A PIECE OF PAPER ON THE TABLE (AND MAKE SURE THAT THERE JUST HAPPENS TO BE A DRINKING STRAW NEARBY). "I'LL EAT MY HAT IF ANYONE CAN PICK UP THE PAPER WITHOUT USING THEIR HANDS... AND KEEPING THE PAPER DRY". (THIS PREVENTS PEOPLE TRYING TO BITE IT UP!) WITH ANY LUCK, YOUR HAT WILL BE SAFE — NO ONE WILL BE ABLE TO DO THIS.

TRY TO KEEP THE SMUG EXPRESSION OFF YOUR CHOPS AS YOU CASUALLY PICK UP THE STRAW, PUT ONE END IN YOUR MOUTH, THE OTHER OVER THE PAPER, AND SUCK HARD.

② RIPPING

TEAR A PIECE OF PAPER LIKE THIS →

THE CHALLENGE IS QUITE STRAIGHTFORWARD:

CAN ANYONE RIP THE PAPER INTO THREE PARTS, HOLDING IT TOP LEFT AND RIGHT? THEY PUFF. THEY HEAVE. THEY SWEAT. ALL TO NO AVAIL. NOW YOU PICK UP THE PAPER, HOLDING IT TOP LEFT AND TOP RIGHT — WITH THE MIDDLE SECTION BETWEEN YOUR TEETH. PULL, AND THE PAPER WILL TEAR INTO THREE PARTS — MUCH TO YOUR FRIENDS' AMAZEMENT.

36

Radar sets in ships can pick up on their screens objects within a radius of 36 miles (58 km).

Queen Elizabeth II is the great-granddaughter thirty-six times removed of Alfred the Great (c.AD 848–900).

An ostrich egg is thirty-six times larger than a hen's egg, and takes rather longer to boil.

Lazy Angler

WHAT HAS THE ANGLER CAUGHT ON EACH OF HIS FISHING LINES?

WHAT DO YOU SEE?

Probably your immediate answer would be, a drawing of a glass. And you would be right, but if you look a little closer, you will discover that you can see something else as well.

THE PALETTE

RE-ARRANGE THE LETTERS TO FIND THE NAMES OF EIGHT COLOURS.

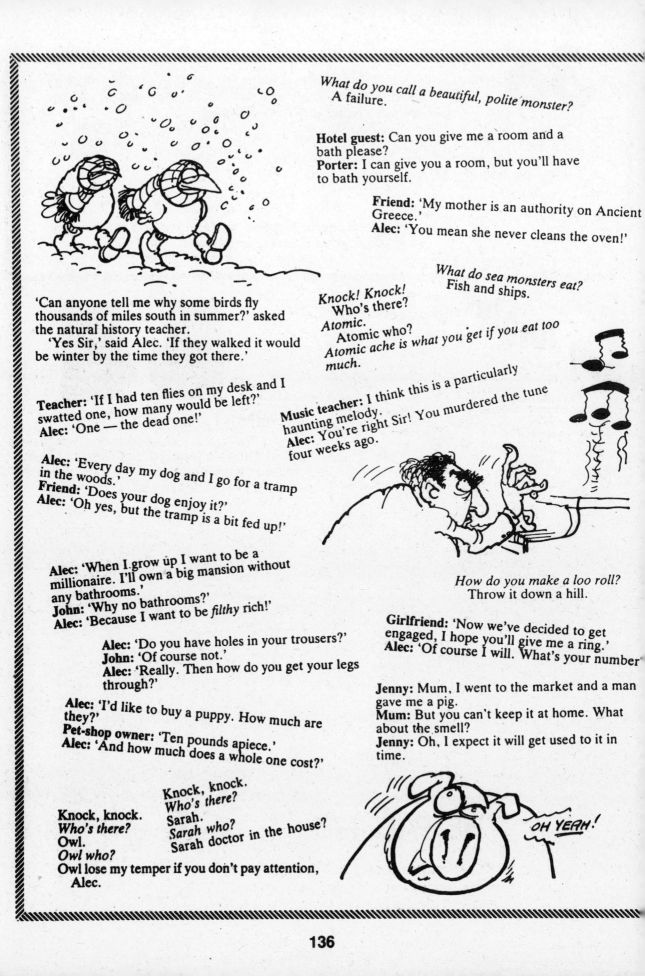

What do you call a beautiful, polite monster?
A failure.

Hotel guest: Can you give me a room and a bath please?
Porter: I can give you a room, but you'll have to bath yourself.

Friend: 'My mother is an authority on Ancient Greece.'
Alec: 'You mean she never cleans the oven!'

What do sea monsters eat?
Fish and ships.

Knock! Knock!
Who's there?
Atomic.
Atomic who?
Atomic ache is what you get if you eat too much.

'Can anyone tell me why some birds fly thousands of miles south in summer?' asked the natural history teacher.
'Yes Sir,' said Alec. 'If they walked it would be winter by the time they got there.'

Teacher: 'If I had ten flies on my desk and I swatted one, how many would be left?'
Alec: 'One — the dead one!'

Music teacher: I think this is a particularly haunting melody.
Alec: You're right Sir! You murdered the tune four weeks ago.

Alec: 'Every day my dog and I go for a tramp in the woods.'
Friend: 'Does your dog enjoy it?'
Alec: 'Oh yes, but the tramp is a bit fed up!'

Alec: 'When I grow up I want to be a millionaire. I'll own a big mansion without any bathrooms.'
John: 'Why no bathrooms?'
Alec: 'Because I want to be *filthy* rich!'

How do you make a loo roll?
Throw it down a hill.

Alec: 'Do you have holes in your trousers?'
John: 'Of course not.'
Alec: 'Really. Then how do you get your legs through?'

Alec: 'I'd like to buy a puppy. How much are they?'
Pet-shop owner: 'Ten pounds apiece.'
Alec: 'And how much does a whole one cost?'

Girlfriend: 'Now we've decided to get engaged, I hope you'll give me a ring.'
Alec: 'Of course I will. What's your number'

Jenny: Mum, I went to the market and a man gave me a pig.
Mum: But you can't keep it at home. What about the smell?
Jenny: Oh, I expect it will get used to it in time.

Knock, knock.
Who's there?
Owl.
Owl who?
Owl lose my temper if you don't pay attention, Alec.

Knock, knock.
Who's there?
Sarah.
Sarah who?
Sarah doctor in the house?

OH YEAH!

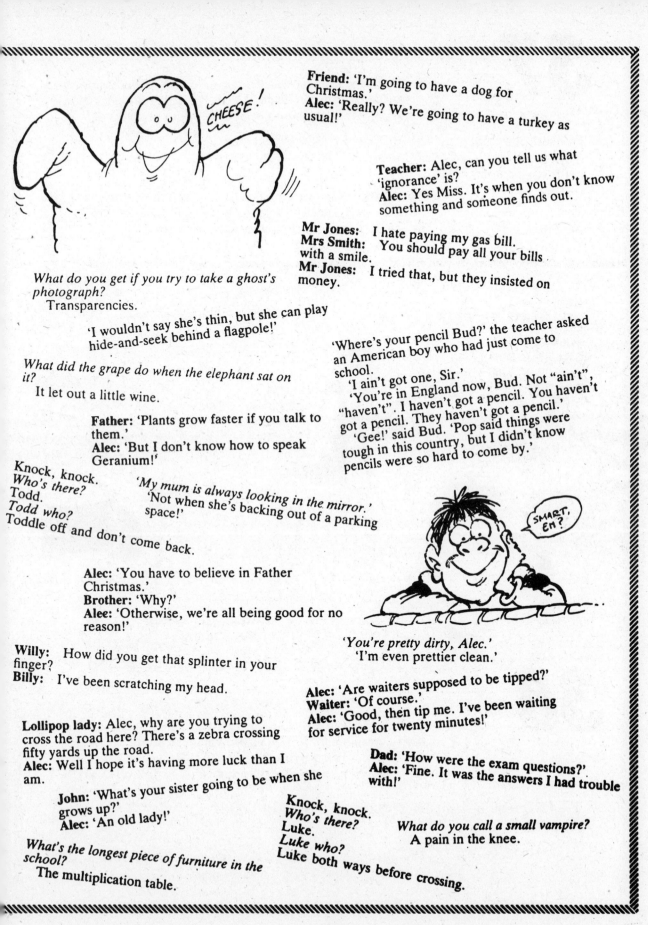

Friend: 'I'm going to have a dog for Christmas.'
Alec: 'Really? We're going to have a turkey as usual!'

Teacher: Alec, can you tell us what 'ignorance' is?
Alec: Yes Miss. It's when you don't know something and someone finds out.

Mr Jones: I hate paying my gas bill.
Mrs Smith: You should pay all your bills with a smile.
Mr Jones: I tried that, but they insisted on money.

What do you get if you try to take a ghost's photograph?
Transparencies.

'I wouldn't say she's thin, but she can play hide-and-seek behind a flagpole!'

What did the grape do when the elephant sat on it?
It let out a little wine.

'Where's your pencil Bud?' the teacher asked an American boy who had just come to school.
'I ain't got one, Sir.'
'You're in England now, Bud. Not "ain't", "haven't". I haven't got a pencil. You haven't got a pencil. They haven't got a pencil.'
'Gee!' said Bud. 'Pop said things were tough in this country, but I didn't know pencils were so hard to come by.'

Father: 'Plants grow faster if you talk to them.'
Alec: 'But I don't know how to speak Geranium!'

Knock, knock.
Who's there?
Todd.
Todd who?
Toddle off and don't come back.

'My mum is always looking in the mirror.'
'Not when she's backing out of a parking space!'

Alec: 'You have to believe in Father Christmas.'
Brother: 'Why?'
Alec: 'Otherwise, we're all being good for no reason!'

'You're pretty dirty, Alec.'
'I'm even prettier clean.'

Willy: How did you get that splinter in your finger?
Billy: I've been scratching my head.

Alec: 'Are waiters supposed to be tipped?'
Waiter: 'Of course.'
Alec: 'Good, then tip me. I've been waiting for service for twenty minutes!'

Lollipop lady: Alec, why are you trying to cross the road here? There's a zebra crossing fifty yards up the road.
Alec: Well I hope it's having more luck than I am.

Dad: 'How were the exam questions?'
Alec: 'Fine. It was the answers I had trouble with!'

John: 'What's your sister going to be when she grows up?'
Alec: 'An old lady!'

Knock, knock.
Who's there?
Luke.
Luke who?
Luke both ways before crossing.

What do you call a small vampire?
A pain in the knee.

What's the longest piece of furniture in the school?
The multiplication table.

37

Between the time he was twenty-nine and his death, thirty-seven years later in 1898, Lewis Carroll (C.L.Dodgson) wrote 98,721 letters and a couple of rather good books!

William Shakespeare (1564–1616) wrote thirty-seven plays, beginning with *Titus Andronicus* in 1594, and concluding with *The Tempest* in 1611.

The Carthaginian general, Hannibal, deployed thirty-seven African elephants to transport heavy goods across the Alps in 218 BC during his campaign against the Romans.

38

The Romney, Hythe and Dymchurch in south-east England – opened in 1927 – is the smallest public railway in the world. Ten locomotives, one-third scale models of famous steam engines, use a gauge of only 38 cm (15 in).

The USA is thirty-eight times bigger in size than the United Kingdom.

The most Golden Discs awarded to an individual were the thirty-eight gained by Elvis Presley (1935–77).

Limerick Fun

The admiral of the fleet
Gave himself a treat.
He went afloat
In a rubber boat
And rowed from Rome to Crete.

Our dog has a cosy box
All lined with cushions and socks.
But he can't eat there,
In his private lair,
It's too sticky from toffee and chocs.

There was a young girl called Sally
Who drove in a big motor rally
On a mountain route
She failed to hoot,
And speedily arrived in the valley!

There was a young gardener from Leeds,
Who swallowed a packet of seeds.
In less than an hour
His nose was a flower
And his head was a bunch of weeds.

There was a young lady of Hove
Who sat down by mistake on a stove;
When they asked, 'Is it hot?'
She replied, 'It is not,'
Said they, 'She's a tough one, by Jove!'

'Mary, Mary, quite contrary,
How does your garden grow?'
'Wilder and wilder,
As the weather gets milder;
It's quite full of weeds, don't you know.'

There was a poor moggie from Hyde,
Who heard that the dog next door had died.
He went through the gate,
And met a terrible fate,
'Cause the cat that had told him had lied!

MATCH THE SHADOW

Study shadow A carefully. Then look over the angry men numbered 1-5. One of them matches shadow A exactly if you placed him in front.

139

PARTY GAMES

SUSAN, JUST LOOK AT THE MESS YOU'RE IN! WHAT **HAVE** YOU BEEN DOING?

I FELL IN A PUDDLE, MUM.

IN YOUR NEW DRESS.

WELL I DIDN'T HAVE TIME TO CHANGE!

SWEET SUCKERS

Fill a large bowl with Smarties and give everyone a saucer and straw. All they have to do is suck a Smartie onto the end of the straw and drop it into the saucers.

The winner is the person who has most sweets in his or her saucer after two minutes. Whoever has this gets to eat all the sweets.

Why couldn't the skeleton go to the disco?

Because he had **nobody** to go with!

KIPPERS

WHOEVER IS 'IT' FACES EVERYONE ELSE, WHO TAKE IT IN TURNS TO FIRE QUESTIONS AT HER NO MATTER WHAT IS ASKED, 'IT' MUST ANSWER 'KIPPERS' WITHOUT THE MEREST HINT OF A SMILE TURNING UP HER LIPS.

IF ANYONE ASKS A QUESTION THAT GETS A SMILE, THAT PERSON TAKES OVER AS 'IT.'

140

39

The thirty-nine books of the Old Testament contain 929 chapters, 23,214 verses, 593,493 words and 2,728,100 letters.

Pliny the Elder (AD 23–79) recorded in his *Natural History* that thirty-nine varieties of pears were known to the Romans.

The teams climb thirty-nine steps at Wembley Stadium to receive the trophy, the medals, the congratulations and commiserations after the annual FA Cup Final.

40

A cricket chirps forty times a minute at temperatures below 10°C (50°F). It increases its rate by four chirps for every degree that the temperature rises.

The hippopotamus, found in East Africa, and the second largest of land mammals, has forty teeth, all appearing to point in different directions!

Rainbows occur only when the sun is below an angle of 40° above the horizon. They are caused by refraction and internal reflection of light in raindrops.

Let's draw a

DOLPHIN

1

2

The dolphin is not a fish, it belongs to the same family as the whale and is a mammal. Dolphins are very clever animals and can be taught many tricks. They have been known to save people from drowning and take them into the shore. Because dolphins are so friendly and are easy to tame, you will find them in many zoos and wild life parks, giving very entertaining shows. In the sea dolphins live together in family groups. If you are on a ship, often a group of dolphins will swim alongside making marvellous leaps in and out of the water.

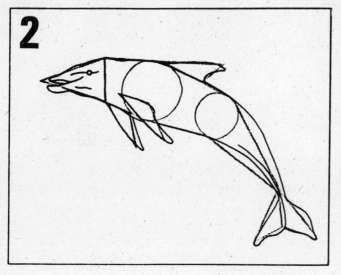

People sometimes think that the tortoise is the same as the turtle. The difference is that tortoises live on land and turtles in the sea. Turtles are also much bigger than tortoises, sometimes as big as 2 metres. Turtles can move very quickly through the water as their feet are shaped like flippers to help them swim. When it is time for the female turtle to lay her eggs, she swims ashore and lays her eggs on the beach. Then she swims away and leaves the young to hatch and find their own way back to the sea. Another difference between turtles and tortoises is that turtles will eat meat and plants, while the tortoise only eats plants. Both the turtle and the tortoise live to a very old age.

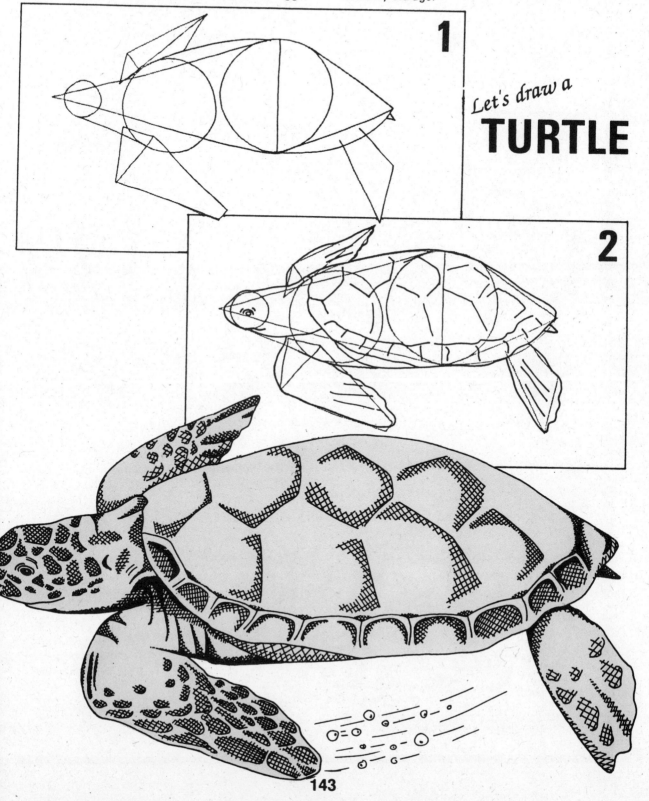

1

Let's draw a
TURTLE

2

'My teacher does bird imitations,' said Alec to Billy.

'What does she do. Whistle like a canary?'

'No. She watches me like a hawk.'

Teacher: Annie. Say something beginning with 'I'.

Annie: I is . . .

Teacher: I *am*, Annie! I am!

Annie: If you say so, Sir. I am the eighth letter of the alphabet.

Mr Anderson, the science master, was very absent-minded. One day he brought a box into the classroom and said, 'I've got a frog and a toad in here. When I get them out we look at the differences.'

He put his hand into the box and pulled two sandwiches.

'Oh dear!' he said. 'I could have sworn just had my lunch.'

NOT YOU AGAIN!

Girlfriend: 'Did your watch stop when you dropped it on the floor?'

Alec: 'Of course! Did you think it would go right through the ground?'

Knock, knock.

Who's there?

Chris.

Chris who?

Christmas comes but once a year.

NEE-DEE RIBET RIBB

'Why are you tearing up your homework notebook and scattering the pieces around the playground?' a furious teacher asked one of her pupils.

'To keep the elephants away, Miss.'

'There are no elephants.'

'Shows how effective it is then, doesn't it?'

Knock, knock.

Who's there?

Maxwell.

Maxwell who?

Mac's well but Annie's poorly.

Knock, knock.

Who's there?

Ida.

Ida who?

I'd a hoe but lost it in the garden.

What exams do horses take at school?

Hay levels.

'What's water, Alec?' asked the science teacher.

'It's a clear colourless liquid that turns black when I put my hands in it.'

'It says on the menu that there's a choice of greens,' said Alec to the dinner lady.

'There is,' said she. 'Broccoli.'

'But that's no choice.'

'Yes it is,' said the dinner lady. 'Take it or leave it.'

What do you call a stupid skeleton?

Bonehead.

Why can't teachers strike pupils with a ruler?

Because the Queen's much too busy to hang around school all day.

For Sale: Large friendly dog. Will eat anything. Very fond of children.

How do you spot a nutter in a car wash?

He's the one on the bicycle.

Teacher: Do you say prayers before meals in your house Alec?
Alec: No Sir . . . Mum's quite a good cook really.

Alec: Please Sir, I've added this column up ten times.
Teacher: Well done Alec; it's always good to check your work before you hand it in.
Alec: Thanks, Sir! Here are my ten answers.

Motorist: Can you tell me the way to Bath?
Local yokel: I always use soap and water.

Knock, knock.
Who's there?
Jim.
Jim who?
J'imagine I'm going to tell you?

Schoolgirl: I'm sorry I missed the goal at hockey Miss. I really could kick myself.
Teacher: Don't bother, Sadie. You'd probably miss.

Knock, knock.
Who's there?
May.
May who?
Made your mistake in asking.

'I don't want to say he's stupid, but when he had to fill out a questionnaire he was stumped on the first line. It said "Name?" '

Sergeant: 'What were you before you joined the army?'
New recruit: 'Happy!'

There was a young lad called Smart Alec
Who grew up into a Dalek.
He went to Dunoon
And there settled doon.
Now Alec, the Dalek, speaks Gaelic.

Alec: 'This soup is terrible.'
Waiter: 'Why do you say that?'
Alec: 'A little swallow told me!'

Knock, knock.
Who's there?
Honor.
Honor who?
On a clear day, you can see forever.

Girlfriend: 'Is it true that carrots improve your sight?'
Alec: 'Have you ever seen a rabbit with glasses?'

What do you get if you eat uranium?
Atomic ache.

'Do you like going to school, Alec?' his grandmother asked.
'I don't mind going,' said Alec. 'And I don't mind coming back. It's the bits in between I don't care for.'

Ivan: 'What do you call a butcher's boy?'
Alec: 'A chop assistant!'

'Doctor, can you give me something for my liver?'
'How about some onions?'

An irate customer in a restaurant complained that his fish was bad, so the waiter picked it up, smacked it and said, 'Naughty, naughty, naughty!'

Teacher: 'Where was the Magna Carta signed?'
Alec: 'At the bottom. Where else?'

Teacher: Can anyone tell me what Gandhi's first name was?
Alec: Goosie, Goosie?

John: 'I've heard that Alaskan dogs can run the fastest.'
Alec: 'It's because the trees are so far apart!'

Teacher: Alec, what's half of eight?
Alec: Up and down, or across Sir?
Teacher: What on earth do you mean?
Alec: Well Sir. Up and down it's 3, and across it's 0.

THAT'S WHY I DON'T LIVE IN ALASKA!

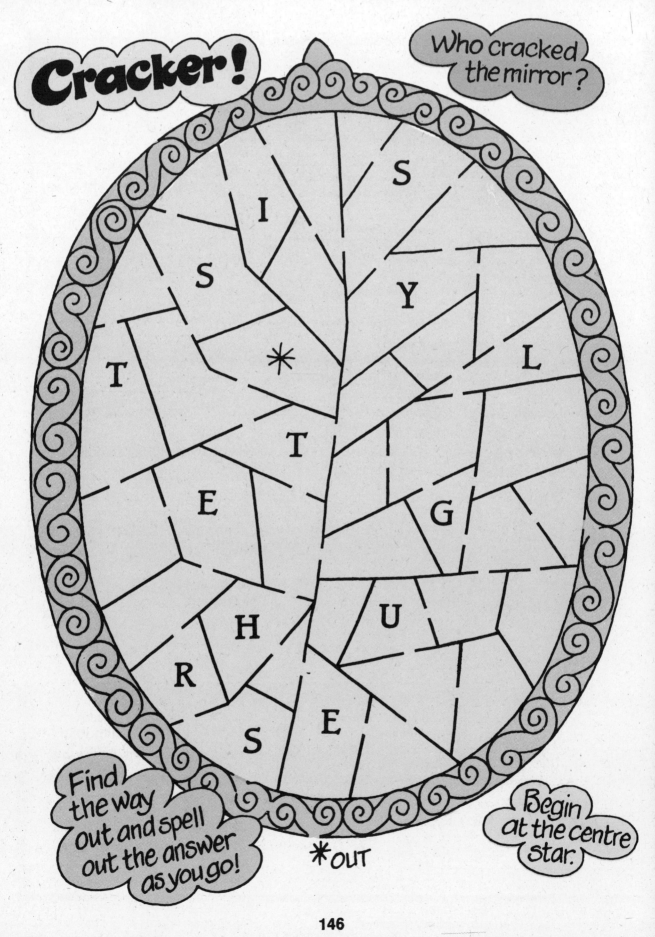

Cracker!

Who cracked the mirror?

Find the way out and spell out the answer as you go!

* OUT

Begin at the centre star.

146

IT TAKES TWO TO PLAY

Ⓐ – TUG O' WAR

You don't need a rope, just strong arms and a friend to pull against. Standing back to back, bend over, put your hands between your legs, grab each other's arms and pull like billy-o.

First to fall over loses that round.

Ⓑ SCISSORS

Face whoever you're playing against, left hand tucked into your trouser band, right hand behind your back. Form your right hand into a 'stone' by making a fist, or 'scissors' by holding your first and second fingers open in a scissor-shape, or 'paper' by keeping your hand open. On the word 'Go', both bring your right hands into view.

PAPER   STONE   SCISSORS

Score as follows:

Scissors cut paper, so a scissor-sign beats an open hand.

Paper wraps stone, so an open hand beats a fist.

Stone blunts scissors, so a fist beats a scissor-sign.

41

Swedish tennis star Björn Borg won forty-one successive matches at Wimbledon before losing the 1981 final to John McEnroe (USA) in four sets. He had won the title for five years in a row.

It takes Mars forty-one minutes longer than it takes Earth to complete its daily rotation.

Forty-one per cent of the Moon's surface is never visible from Earth. Only twenty-one American astronauts have seen the hidden side.

Night of Horror

by Robert Moss

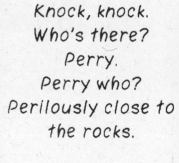

Knock, knock.
Who's there?
Perry.
Perry who?
Perilously close to
the rocks.

Where is the English
channel, Alec?
asked the
geography teacher.
Don't ask me, Sir,
said Alec. We can
only get BBC1 on
our television.

"Don't mistake me, good Stubbs," said Pesky, "I have every respect for the Swan of Avon —"

"The Swan of Avon?" repeated Stubbs, puzzled. "I know the Fleece and the George at —"

Pesky groaned. "The Swan of Avon is not a hotel, Stubbs. It is not a *what* but a *who*. The Swan of Avon is the Immortal Bard, the Sweet Singer of Stratford, the imperishable playwright, the great poet of humanity — in a word, Stubbs, William Shakespeare. You have heard of him, I presume?"

"Don't be silly, of course I have! He wrote *The Merchant of Venice* and *Hamlet* and *Macbeth*, and that thing they made into a musical — *Pyg*-something."

"*Pygmalion*, Stubbs," said Pesky, wincing, "is indisputably the work of George Bernard Shaw. There may be some

> Can anyone give me an example of a double negative? asked the English teacher. Alec?
> I don't know none, Sir.
> Excellent.
>
> What lies in a cot and wobbles?
> A jelly baby.

doubt of the authorship of Shakespeare's plays, but I have never heard it claimed that he wrote *Pygmalion*."

"Well, you never know," said Stubbs obstinately.

Pesky sighed. "In this case our knowledge is complete," he assured his chum. "But let it pass. Shakespeare, who was never really happy unless he had three or four corpses lying about the stage and a mad woman screaming in the wings, is deemed by our unmentionable Head to be fit for schoolboys to act, but horror films are taboo."

"It isn't fair," agreed Stubbs.

"Why," continued Pesky, "shouldn't we be horrified the same as adults? It's just another example of the Trumpet's tyranny, Stubbs. Even if he doesn't want to see a man who hasn't got a face, that's no reason why he should stop us from seeing it."

"Of course it isn't," agreed Stubbs. "He's a killjoy."

"But mark you," went on Pesky, warming to his subject, "it isn't only the Trumpet we're up against; it's the whole of the adult world, you might say. They give a film an over-18 certificate, so that even if the Headmaster isn't against chaps seeing it, they still keep us out."

"As if our money isn't as good as anybody else's," agreed Stubbs indignantly.

"On the rare occasions that we have any, it certainly is." Pesky paused and looked hopefully at his chum. "You don't happen to have any on you, do you, Stubby? I fancy an

> What music do bulls like best?
> Cow-lypso music.
>
> What's as big as an elephant, but doesn't weigh anything?
> His shadow.
>
> How can you tell if there's an elephant under your bed?
> Your nose touches the ceiling.
>
> What has big ears and hops?
> An elephant on a pogo stick.

ice-cream or a lemonade."

Stubbs shook his head glumly. "Not a bean," he admitted, "till Friday."

Pesky shook his head mournfully. "Things are pretty grim at the Towers these days."

They strolled on in silence.

Dr Trump, headmaster of the Towers School, had expressed himself forcefully that morning on the subject of unwholesome films, and pointed out the educational and cultural superiority of the plays of William Shakespeare over the rubbishy horror films currently being shown on the cinema screen for the edification of the cinema-going public. So carried away had Dr Trump been that he ended by announcing that for the end-of-term play one of Shakespeare's masterpieces would be selected.

How do you get down from an elephant? You don't. You get down from a swan.

Where do jungle animals eat? At a beastro.

Pesky, who seldom found himself in agreement with Dr Trump on any subject, feared that he would be pressed into the cast of Shakespearean players and be compelled to spend laborious hours learning lines. By the same token, the horror film advertised to be shown at the Pavilion Cinema in the adjoining town of Beckstead began to exert a magnetic attraction for him since being vigorously denounced by Dr Trump and banned.

"By George, Stubby!" he breathed, halting before a hoarding on the seafront of Prettywell-on-Sea — a village seaside resort close to the Towers — along which they were sauntering. "Doesn't it look absolutely plus and super?"

Stubbs looked at the poster and sucked in his breath sharply.

"It's a wow!" he muttered simply.

The poster showed a man with a green-tinted hand covering that portion of his body where his face would have been if he'd had a face — which, according to the title and the other sinister yellow wording on the poster, he hadn't. The advertisement went on to pledge that if you saw this monstrous and terrible film you couldn't fail to awake screaming in the night, go about even in broad daylight looking apprehensively over your shoulder, and generally find your hitherto satisfactory nervous system ravaged and shattered, perhaps for ever.

"Gosh, what wouldn't I give to see it!" said Stubbs enviously.

Pesky nodded. "The fact that Beckstead is out of bounds wouldn't matter. What we can't get over, though, is that miserable over-18 certificate. We'd never pass for adults, and they're terribly strict at cinemas these days."

"I should have thought you'd have found a way," said Stubbs.

Pesky put a hand on his shoulder. "I'm touched by your faith in me, Stubby. Maybe I will, even yet. I —" He broke off suddenly and whisked Stubbs with a quick movement into a convenient shelter that stood close by. "It's Twinkle," he explained. "Better not let him see us, or ten to one he'll think of a part for us in the play."

Mr Starr, otherwise Twinkle, a master at the Towers, had been named as producer of the school's next play. Pesky

Why did the flea fail his O levels?
He wasn't up to scratch.

How can you tell if an elephant's in your fridge?
The door won't shut.

There was a young wife from Uganda,
Renowned for her coolness and candour.
When, during abuse,
Someone said, You goose!
She quickly retorted, Uganda!

Knock, knock.
Who's there?
Hermes.
Hermes who?
Her measles are very catching.

Ballet Teacher: Alec, What's an entrechat?
Alec: A cat-flap, Miss?

and Stubbs knew little of Mr Starr, who had only come to the school at the beginning of the current term, but what little they did know hadn't given them the impression that Mr Starr would make school a place of sweetness, sunshine and light.

Unfortunately, Mr Starr had a keen eye and spotted both boys before they dodged into the shelter.

"Ah, Pesky and Stubbs!" he called out with what struck Pesky and Stubbs as deceitful heartiness. "Just the boys I'm looking for!"

Reluctantly, the two emerged from cover, pretending to be surprised, not to say gratified, at the sight of the master.

"I am in the process of casting our play, Pesky and Stubbs, which Dr Trump and I have decided will be *Julius Caesar*. I think you would make two very good conspirators, eh? You have a conspiratorial air about you just now — ha, ha! And while Stubbs here could hardly be said to have a lean and hungry Cassius look I don't doubt that we shall be able to find a part to fit his particular type of looks — eh, Stubbs?"

Stubbs gave the master a sickly smile.

"As you seem to be proceeding along the promenade somewhat aimlessly, Pesky and Stubbs, it will not inconvenience you, I am sure, to return with me to the school to discuss the play and the cast in some detail, eh?"

"Not at all, sir," replied Pesky, who knew when he was trapped. "*Julius Caesar* is an excellent choice, sir, I think — far better than *The Man Without a Face*, sir."

"The what?" said Mr Starr.

Pesky pointed to the poster, which they had just reached. "One of those unwholesome horror films that Dr Trump was warning us against this morning, sir." He shuddered. "Quite revolting, don't you think, sir?"

"Yes, of course — most." Mr Starr was gazing at the poster as if fascinated. "As you say, Pesky, quite revolting. 'A monstrous and terrible film . . .'" he muttered, reading the wording on the poster. "'Wake screaming in the night . . . makes the flesh creep!' Good gracious! What was that you were saying, Pesky?"

"I was remarking what a fine wholesome play *Julius Caesar* is, sir. I believe Caesar is stabbed from behind in the

152

first act, isn't he, sir — foully murdered?"

"Eh? Yes, indeed, Pesky, but of course murder in a Shakespeare play is in — er — a different category from this kind of — er — rubbish. But come; let us get back to the school and begin planning our production."

The next two hours were an unrelieved bore to Stubbs, but Pesky, to his chum's surprise, was humming cheerfully when the meeting finally broke up.

"I've solved the problem, good Stubbs. All we need to see *The Man Without a Face* is the price of a couple of seats and moustaches to suit our hair colouring."

"Moustaches?" exclaimed Stubbs, startled.

"Unless you prefer a beard." Pesky stepped back and regarded him critically. "Perhaps you would look better in a beard, Stubby — the bristly type, to go with your square face and bullet head."

"What d'you mean — square face and bullet head?" cried Stubbs indignantly. "And what's this you're burbling about a beard?"

"There's nothing like a bit of face fungus to make a chap

look old and crusted, friend Stubbs. A bushy black moustache for me, a scrubby ginger beard for you, and the cinema will fling wide its gilded doors to us."

"What!" muttered Stubbs, awed. "You mean – ?"

"What is the use of joining a distinguished cast of moustached and bearded Shakespearean players if you can't turn it to personal advantage, good Stubby? All that remains for us to do in order to have the privilege of awaking screaming in the night is to choose our moustaches, beg, borrow or appropriate a couple of hats, and raise the price of admission. In fact, I'm inclined to think the last will be the hardest of all."

"I say!" breathed Stubbs. "You mean, borrow from the Shakespeare make-up stuff?"

"Exactly," smiled Pesky. "A moustache for me, a beard

for you – and there's nothing to stand between us and the man without a face, except a few paltry coins for the seats, and that, good Stubbs, we will not allow to stand in our way."

"I say!" breathed Stubbs. "I say, Pesky, you're a blessed genius, no less!"

The following evening two figures, one tall, one short and stocky, might have been seen scaling the wall of the Towers School at a spot where a tall elm cast a deep shadow. The evening was dark and the weather rough, so much so that the tall figure felt a warning was desirable.

"It's blowing half a gale, Stubby, so watch your hat doesn't blow off."

"It isn't my hat I'm worried about," returned Stubbs. "It's my beard. It nearly went in that last gust of wind."

"For heaven's sake, man, grip on to it," urged Pesky, alarmed. "Remember, no beard, no film. By George, confound it!"

"What's up?" demanded Stubbs.

"My moustache – it's gone!"

"What?" Stubbs gazed in dismay. Then he grinned. "It isn't gone, old man – it's just mislaid! It's up by your eye."

I told you to get a haircut yesterday, said the headmaster to Alec.
I did Sir, said Alec.
That one.

Alec: Please Sir! Can I be excused to go and get a glass of water?
Teacher: You've had five in the last ten minutes, Alec.
Alec: I know but the fire in the wastepaper basket is still burning.

Which side of a sheep has the most wool?
The outside.

There was a young woman from Looe
Who dreamt she was eating her shoe.
She awoke in the night
In a terrible fright,
To find it was perfectly true.

Reaching out, he plucked the false moustache from over Pesky's cheek and returned it to his upper lip. "Remember what you said – no moustache, no film. So grip on to it."

Pesky grunted. "We'll be all right when we're out of this wind. Here's the Beckstead bus coming. Keep your head; this is our first test."

To the gratification of the two masqueraders, no one in the bus took any special notice of them. As Pesky remarked, it hurt to have to pay full fare on the bus, instead of enjoying the schoolboy privilege of half fare but, at any rate, it showed that their disguise was passable.

At the cinema they had to join a long queue, but this proved to be an advantage, for the cashier at the box-office was too busy issuing tickets to spare more than a glance at the customers.

Within a few minutes the two were in the safe darkness of the cinema, struggling along a packed row of seats to two vacant ones.

"Done it, Stubby!" whispered Pesky jubilantly, as he sank with relief into a seat. "Done it without a hitch!"

"Now for *The Man Without a Face!*" said Stubbs, with relish.

For the next ninety minutes the two sat in pleasurable horror gazing at the forbidden film, at the end of which Pesky announced that it was definitely one of those films that had to be seen twice for the full flavour of it to be enjoyed. Stubbs agreed with this sentiment but claimed that the full flavour could only be realized in conjunction with an ice-cream.

"An ice-cream let it be, then, good Stubbs," agreed Pesky heartily.

As the lights went up for the interval, Stubbs struggled into the gangway and returned with two ice-creams, which Pesky gazed upon with undisguised pleasure. Stubbs, however, soon found that a bushy beard was a severe handicap when eating ice-cream. Finally, in desperation, he jerked the beard aside in order to allow unobstructed entry to the ice-cream.

This, however, was too much for a stout woman two seats away whose nerves had already been frayed to breaking point by the man without a face. Turning her head towards Stubbs just as he held the beard aside with one

> Knock, knock.
> Who's there?
> Van.
> Van who?
> Van I vant yu, I'll call.
>
> What kind of apes talk a lot?
> Blab-boons.
>
> Did you hear the one about the scientist who crossed a cat with a gorilla? He got an animal that puts him out at night!
>
> Where does a ten ton gorilla sleep? Anywhere it wants.

> Did you hear the story about the two weevils? One worked hard and got ahead in life. The other didn't and remained the lesser of two weevils.

hand while popping a spoonful of ice-cream into his mouth with the other, she let out a piercing, terrified scream, which froze her neighbours, including Pesky and Stubbs, in their seats.

As an usherette hurried towards her, she gestured accusingly at Pesky and Stubbs. "He's got a – he took –" she began hysterically.

Pesky leaned forward. "The film, you know," he told the usherette smoothly. "It rather upsets some people – a trifle bloodcurdling, if you see what I mean."

The usherette nodded, and took the stout woman by the arm. "Let me help you out, dearie," she murmured.

Murmuring incoherently, the stout woman permitted herself to be led out and up the gangway. Pesky leaned towards Stubbs and jerked his beard into place. "Wipe the ice-cream off it, Stubby," he urged. Then: "Oh jeepers!"

With goggling eyes he watched a second usherette point with her torch at the seat just vacated by the stout woman.

"Don't look now," he breathed to Stubbs, "but Twinkle's coming to sit by us."

"Twinkle!" Stubbs gasped the word out.

Pesky pressed a hand to his bearded lips and hissed, "Shurrup!"

"It's Twinkle!" he whispered in Stubbs' ear as the lights winked out again. "And he's between us and the gangway!"

"What in blazes is Twinkle doing here?" demanded Stubbs aggressively.

"It could be, good Stubbs, that our Twinkle is a hypocrite, an imposter, a masquerader, one who pretends a liking for the aesthetic and cultural while all the time cherishing a low taste for the sensational and horrific."

"Like us, you mean?"

"Are we hypocrites, imposters, masqueraders, Stubbs?"

"Yes – no! I mean we're wearing beards – or, at least, I am, and the wretched thing itches."

Murmurs of displeasure from patrons behind and beside them forced the two into silence.

Pesky, however, could no longer give his undivided attention to the film. His mind was exercised by a problem that became more pressing every minute. The problem was, how could he and Stubbs get out of the cinema in time to catch the last bus home? He had calculated everything to a nicety, but the arrival of Mr Starr threw all his carefully laid plans into disorder.

If Mr Starr stayed until the end of the film, which was extremely likely, Pesky and Stubbs would miss the bus home and be faced with a walk of not less than five weary miles. On the other hand, if they attempted to rise and reach the gangway in the middle of the film they would undoubtedly draw attention to themselves, probably provoke murmurs of discontent among their neighbours, and – much, much worse – be recognized by Twinkle in the very act of passing him, for, as Pesky reminded himself, Mr Starr possessed a pair of eyes that a hawk on the wing might envy.

"We've got to get out before the bus goes, though," Pesky told himself. "The only way I can see is to make for the other gangway."

With a whispered word into Stubbs' ear, he rose and began to make his way towards the gangway in the opposite direction to Mr Starr.

"Hey, you go t'other way – go on!" murmured his next-door neighbour threateningly. "You don't need to come

Where do sheep go for haircuts?
To the baa baa shop.

Finding a maggot in your apple is not as bad as finding only half a maggot.

Lamb is sheep at any price but venison is always deer.

Is this river good for fish?
It must be, said the angler. I can't get any of them to leave.

Knock, knock.
Who's there?
Stanislas.
Stanislas who?
Stan is last up every morning.

What do you get if you cross a Dobermann with a werewolf?
A very nervous postman.

past me to get out."

A heavy finger poked Pesky in the back, and the owner of the finger, seated in the row behind, said, "Sit down, can't you, or get out!"

All things considered, especially the prospect of a five-mile walk if they missed the bus, Pesky decided that the time had come to take a chance.

"Keep your face away from Twinkle," he breathed into Stubbs' ear. "If he spots us we'll be confined to barracks for weeks."

Stubbs nodded.

Muttering apologies, Pesky led the way to the gangway. As they squeezed past him, Mr Starr glanced up at them, and a flicker of incredulity came into his eyes. As they hurried up the gangway towards the exit, his eyes followed them.

> The teacher explained, Quite a number of plants and flowers have the prefix 'dog'. The dog rose is one, but there are many more. She asked, Who can name another? I can, shouted a student. Collie-flower.

> A young boy walked into a pet shop and asked if there were any dogs going cheap. The wiseguy salesman said, Sorry, kid, all our dogs go woof.
>
> Please Miss, said Andrea. Yesterday my cat fell from a tree that was over 100 feet tall. Was she hurt? asked the worried teacher. Not really, said Andrea. She only climbed up about two feet.

"No, no, it can't be!" he muttered. Then suddenly, as if making up his mind, he rose from his seat and made his way swiftly towards the exit. He was just in time to see Pesky and Stubbs haring it towards a bus that stood waiting in the road. He broke into a run.

Pesky reached the bus, stood aside to let Stubbs get on, then glanced back at the figure he could see setting off from the cinema in what looked suspiciously like pursuit.

Pesky, the hero of many a narrow squeak, did not panic. Calmly, he said to Stubbs, "Up them stairs, Stubby, and keep your hairy face down. Twinkle is 'ot on our 'eels."

"My stars!" muttered Stubbs. "If he catches us there'll be fireworks!"

"Nevertheless, good Stubbs," said Pesky, sinking down in a seat on the top deck beside his chum, "I shall have one or two pertinent — not to say impertinent — questions to put to the starry Twinkle."

"Questions? Such as?"

"What are you doing, good Twinkle, in a cinema showing such a depraving film as *The Man Without a Face*?"

"He's a master; he can go where he pleases," Stubbs pointed out.

"True, but we might occasion him some embarrassment during the process of going to gaol," Pesky pointed out. "We shall not take it lying down, Stubby. He will not come out of the encounter unscathed."

Had they but known it, Mr Starr was already scathed. About to put a firm foot on the platform of the bus, he found himself looking at a large hand pitted with bell-ringing marks.

"Full up!" said a loud, authoritative voice. "Full right up!"

"That's all right," said Mr Starr. "I will stand."

"Not in this bus, you won't mate. We're full up. You eard. Five standin' inside, an' that's the lot."

"I protest," said Mr Starr. "I have five miles to go. I can't walk that distance. I —"

"You shouldn't stay out so late at night, then, should you?"

The conductor gave three hearty bangs on the bell, and the bus began to move. Hastily, Mr Starr dropped off.

Peering out of the window, Stubbs beheld the figure of the master standing in the road gazing after the bus.

"By gosh!" he said. "He's been left behind!"

"There is a providence that shapes our ends, good Stubby, rough-hew them how we may," murmured Pesky. "I forget who said that; it wasn't Shakespeare."

"It must have been Omar what's-his-name — you know, the chap who was in the wilderness with a book and a bottle of wine." Stubbs' tone was jovial.

Teacher: Alec! Why are you panting so hard?
Alec: I've been running up the road to stop a fight.
Teacher: That's very brave. Who was fighting?
Alec: Me and Billy Bridges.

Knock, knock.
Who's there?
Duke.
Duke who?
Duke come here often?

Teacher: Alec, I told you to write a hundred times 'I must do better in arithmetic'. You've only done 75. Why?
Alec: I'd have thought that was fairly obvious, Sir.

Teacher: Alec! Give me one use for goat-skin.
Alec: It holds the goat together.

"I know who you mean, but it wasn't him," said Pesky. "Whoever it was must have had us in mind when he wrote it."

"But how could he?" demanded Stubbs, frowning in puzzlement. "He wouldn't know us or anything about us. I don't see —"

"Skip it," urged Pesky. "The point is of trifling importance. Let us instead rejoice, good Stubby, that we have had our evening out, our fill of horror, nausea and degradation, and now need only sit back and enjoy the scenery."

"I can't see much scenery," said Stubbs, peering out of the window. "It's dark outside."

"Then let us enjoy the scenery within!" said Pesky happily. "Or, rather, you can; I'm going to have a brief, refreshing sleep, as the hour is late. Wake me, good Stubbs, when we reach our destination."

Pesky closed his eyes and slept, while the faithful Stubbs

kept vigil, dutifully waking his chum when the school stop was reached. Yawning gently, Pesky led the way back over the wall and by devious means into the school and their dormitory.

"A most successful evening," said Pesky, as he climbed into bed. "I have a fancy that you may like to join me in, good Stubbs. I propose to excite in our esteemed but unadventurous dormitory mates a quiver of curiosity in the morning. I shall sleep in my moustache tonight."

Stubbs chuckled. "I'm with you! Won't they stare?"

So, as the two lay back and closed their eyes, an observer looking into the dormitory would have seen an odd sight – a row of single beds, each with a boy occupant, but one of them wearing a moustache on his upper lip and the other with a ginger beard laid neatly on the outside of the sheet.

There was an old man from Carlisle,
Who sat down one day on a stile.
The paint it was wet,
So he's sitting there yet;
But he hopes to get off with a file!

Fortunately, Mr Starr was too weary to take a look into the dormitory. In fact, he hadn't yet reached the school. He was out on the road – and he still had two and a half miles to do . . .

1

Kangaroos are very strange animals. When they want to move, they do not run or walk like most animals. They jump in the air on their two very strong back legs. Another strange thing about kangaroos is that they carry their young in a pouch on their stomachs. The young live in these pouches for a long time until they are strong enough to come out and look for their own food. The kangaroo eats grass and leaves and its legs are so strong that, if attacked by another animal the kangaroo could easily kick hard enough to kill it.

Let's draw a
KANGAROO

2

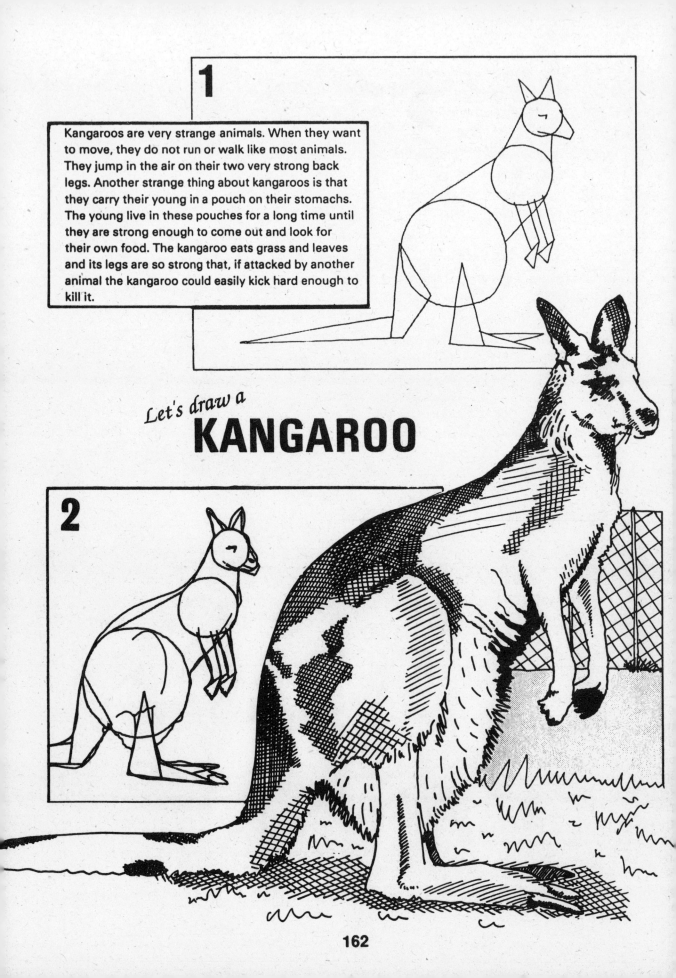

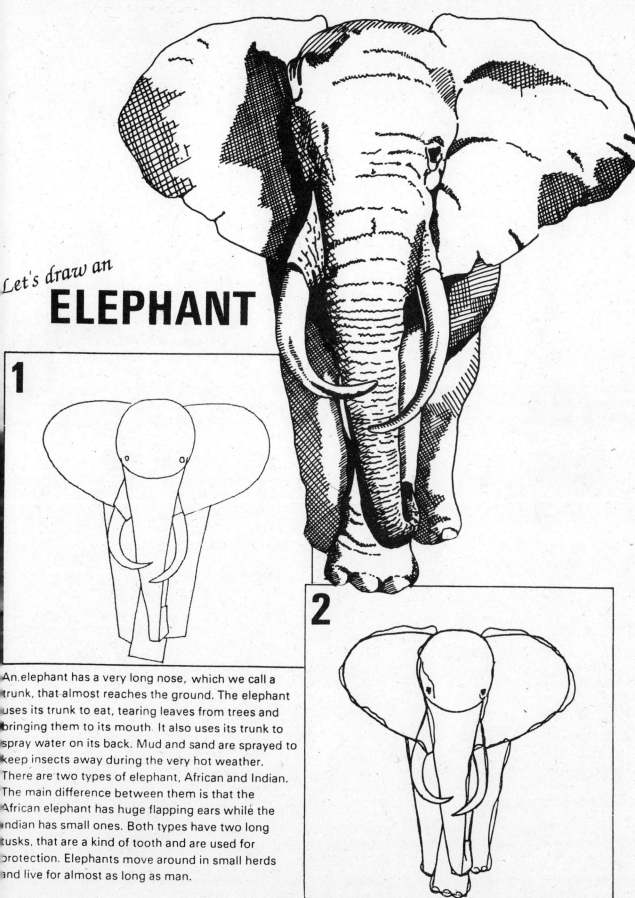

Let's draw an
ELEPHANT

1

2

An elephant has a very long nose, which we call a trunk, that almost reaches the ground. The elephant uses its trunk to eat, tearing leaves from trees and bringing them to its mouth. It also uses its trunk to spray water on its back. Mud and sand are sprayed to keep insects away during the very hot weather. There are two types of elephant, African and Indian. The main difference between them is that the African elephant has huge flapping ears while the Indian has small ones. Both types have two long tusks, that are a kind of tooth and are used for protection. Elephants move around in small herds and live for almost as long as man.

42

The beam from Ptolemy I's lighthouse (260 BC) on the island of Pharos, off Alexandria in Egypt, could be seen from a distance of 42 miles (67.6 km). Truly a wonder!

Napoleon was placed forty-second in a class of fifty-one as he scraped through military school at Brienne in 1785. He was sixteen years old.

A silkworm will feed for forty-two days before spinning a cocoon. By that time it will have eaten twenty times its own weight of mulberry leaves.

All around

Fit the picture names into the circle

SPOT THE TWINS

Can you find the two identical men?

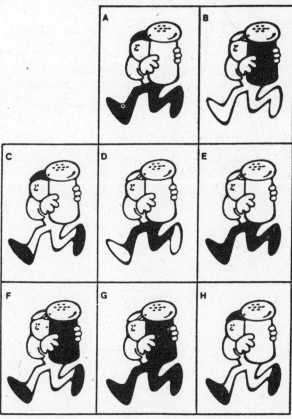

PICTURE SUMS

Can you work out the value of each tool?

$+ = 60_p$ $+ = 80_p$ $+ = 100_p$

Paper and Pencil Games

① BOXES

THIS SIMPLE GAME FOR TWO PLAYERS IS GREAT FUN AND ALSO QUITE SKILFUL.

DRAW SEVEN LINES VERY LIGHTLY ON A PIECE OF PAPER AND DOT THEM LIKE THIS,

PLAYERS TAKE IT IN TURNS TO DRAW A LINE CONNECTING EITHER VERTICAL OR HORIZONTAL DOTS. THE AIM IS TO COMPLETE MORE BOXES THAN YOUR OPPONENT. OBVIOUSLY YOU HAVE TO BE CAREFUL NOT TO DRAW A THIRD SIDE TO A BOX, AS THIS LEAVES A FINISHING CHANCE FOR THE OTHER PLAYER. WHEN A PLAYER COMPLETES A BOX, HE PUTS HIS INITIAL INSIDE AND HAS ANOTHER TURN.

② DANCERS

Each player has a piece of paper and a pencil. You also need a dice. A six starts the game.

Players try to complete a dancer, using the code below to draw in various parts of the body, according to the number thrown. Start with the TRUNK. You must have arms before you can add hands, legs before feet, and a face before finishing off the eyes, nose and mouth.

6 = TRUNK

5 = HEAD

4 = ARMS & LEGS

3 = HANDS or FEET

2 = EYES

1 = NOSE & MOUTH

166

43

Even faster than the greyhound is the remarkable saluki, which has been timed at 43 mph (69 kph). It was used as a hunting dog in ancient Egypt.

The stories of Sherlock Holmes have now appeared in forty-three languages, as well as Esperanto, Braille and even shorthand.

Arid and semi-arid areas now cover 43 per cent of the land surface of the world. The average daytime temperature in the Sahara desert is 43°C (110°F).

Limerick Fun

A man from Inverness
Always looks a mess.
His shirt is torn,
His jacket's worn,
And his trousers need a press.

A tutor who taught on the flute,
Tried to teach two young tooters to toot.
Said the two to the tutor:
'Is it harder to toot, or
To tutor two tooters to toot?'

Little Bo-peep has lost her sheep
And I know where to find them:
In the deep-freeze,
With packs of peas
Stacked up neatly behind them.

An elephant born in Tibet,
One day in its cage wouldn't get.
So its keeper stood near,
Stuck a hose in its ear,
And invented the first Jumbo Jet.

I know a fellow named Will,
Who objects to being called Bill.
His behaviour is silly
If called 'Billy' or 'Willy';
And 'William' makes him feel ill.

A curious fish is the chub,
Framed on the wall of a pub.
It took some bait
It shouldn't have ate,
And got hooked on the wrong sort of grub!

A housewife called Christina
Could hardly be much meaner.
She'll use a cat
To beat her mat,
Not a vacuum-cleaner!

SIX DIFFERENCES

There are 6 differences between the two pictures. How quickly can you find them?

Memory Test

Study the picture for 30 seconds, then give the book to your friend and let him ask you the following questions.

1. How many holes are there in the hose?
2. Does the fireman have a moustache?
3. Is there a pocket in his coat?
4. Does the fireman have gloves on?
5. Are his shoes black?

IN SPAIN

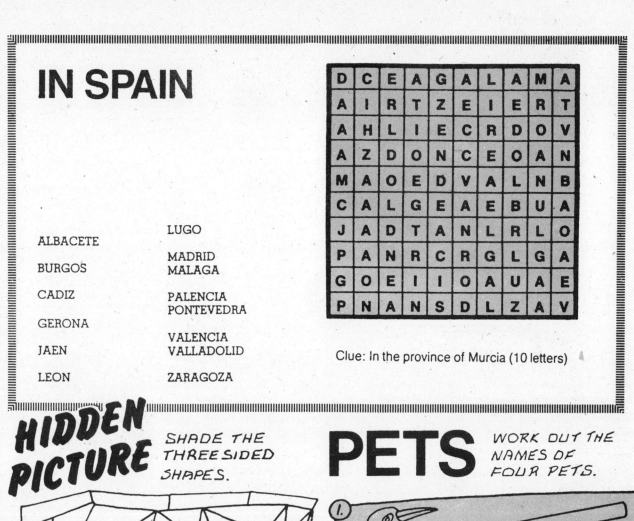

D	C	E	A	G	A	L	A	M	A
A	I	R	T	Z	E	I	E	R	T
A	H	L	I	E	C	R	D	O	V
A	Z	D	O	N	C	E	O	A	N
M	A	O	E	D	V	A	L	N	B
C	A	L	G	E	A	E	B	U	A
J	A	D	T	A	N	L	R	L	O
P	A	N	R	C	R	G	L	G	A
G	O	E	I	I	O	A	U	A	E
P	N	A	N	S	D	L	Z	A	V

ALBACETE

BURGOS

CADIZ

GERONA

JAEN

LEON

LUGO

MADRID
MALAGA

PALENCIA
PONTEVEDRA

VALENCIA
VALLADOLID

ZARAGOZA

Clue: In the province of Murcia (10 letters)

HIDDEN PICTURE
SHADE THE THREE SIDED SHAPES.

PETS
WORK OUT THE NAMES OF FOUR PETS.

169

After his defeat by Cromwell's Roundheads at Worcester in 1653, Charles II became a fugitive, and for forty-four days he was hunted throughout England before managing to escape to France from Shoreham, Sussex.

Starfish usually have five arms, but one species has forty-four.

In 1710, some forty-four years after the Great Fire of London, Sir Christopher Wren's masterpiece, St Paul's Cathedral, was finally completed.

CHEEKY CHALLENGES

a knotty problem

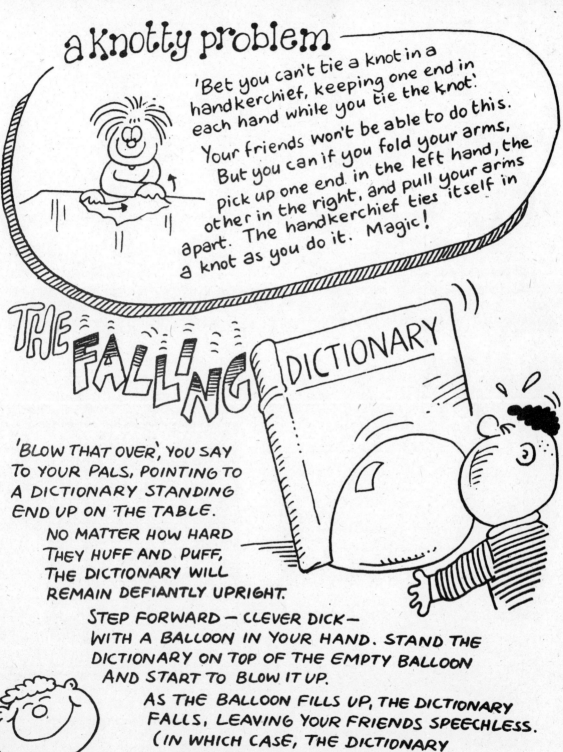

'Bet you can't tie a knot in a handkerchief, keeping one end in each hand while you tie the knot!

Your friends won't be able to do this. But you can if you fold your arms, pick up one end in the left hand, the other in the right, and pull your arms apart. The handkerchief ties itself in a knot as you do it. Magic!

THE FALLING DICTIONARY

'BLOW THAT OVER', YOU SAY TO YOUR PALS, POINTING TO A DICTIONARY STANDING END UP ON THE TABLE.

NO MATTER HOW HARD THEY HUFF AND PUFF, THE DICTIONARY WILL REMAIN DEFIANTLY UPRIGHT.

STEP FORWARD — CLEVER DICK — WITH A BALLOON IN YOUR HAND. STAND THE DICTIONARY ON TOP OF THE EMPTY BALLOON AND START TO BLOW IT UP.

AS THE BALLOON FILLS UP, THE DICTIONARY FALLS, LEAVING YOUR FRIENDS SPEECHLESS. (IN WHICH CASE, THE DICTIONARY SHOULD COME IN HANDY!)

PLAY CHESS

CHECKMATE

FIANCHETTO

GAME

HORSE

KING
KNIGHT

MATCH
MOVE

OPPONENT

PAWN
POSITION
PRODIGY

QUEEN

RANK
ROOK

SKILL
STRATEGY

S	T	R	A	T	E	G	Y	K	F
P	O	S	I	T	I	O	N	I	I
V	I	T	H	G	I	N	K	N	A
Y	C	P	G	M	O	V	E	G	N
G	E	T	A	M	K	C	E	H	C
I	N	T	M	W	R	O	S	R	H
D	E	R	E	Y	N	O	R	A	E
O	E	M	A	T	C	H	O	N	T
R	U	L	L	I	K	S	H	K	T
P	Q	T	N	E	N	O	P	P	O

Clue: Success (7 letters)

45

The most famous of America's early gunsmiths was Samuel Colt (1814–62). The Colt 45, a heavy duty automatic pistol, perpetuates his name.

The Nile crocodile has forty-five changes of teeth before it is fully grown!

There are 45,000 species and varieties of plants in the Royal Botanical Gardens at Kew, first opened to the public in 1841.

TREES

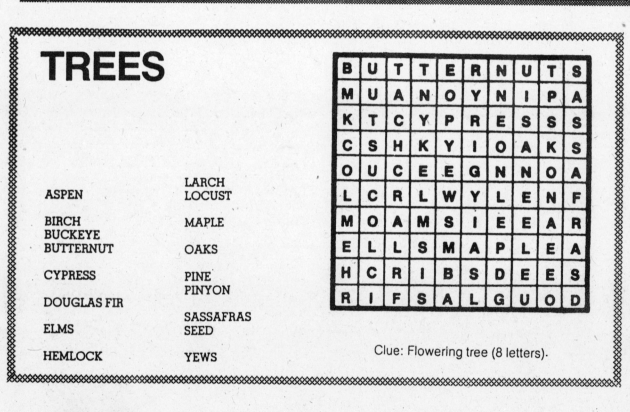

ASPEN

BIRCH
BUCKEYE
BUTTERNUT

CYPRESS

DOUGLAS FIR

ELMS

HEMLOCK

LARCH
LOCUST

MAPLE

OAKS

PINE
PINYON

SASSAFRAS
SEED

YEWS

Clue: Flowering tree (8 letters).

46

There are forty-six Doric columns, each over 9.15 m (30 ft) high, in the Parthenon, the magnificent building dating from ancient times which dominates the Greek capital of Athens.

A Spanish guitar normally has six strings and nineteen rests, and can produce forty-six different notes.

The Duke of Wellington and Napoleon Bonaparte, his adversary at Waterloo in 1815, were both forty-six at the time.

Sid's Picture Puzzle

FILL IN THE GRID, USING THE PICTURE CLUES,
AND ONE OF THE VERTICAL COLUMNS WILL GIVE YOU
A LONG WORD. (IT'S SO LONG, SID CAN'T EVEN SAY IT!)

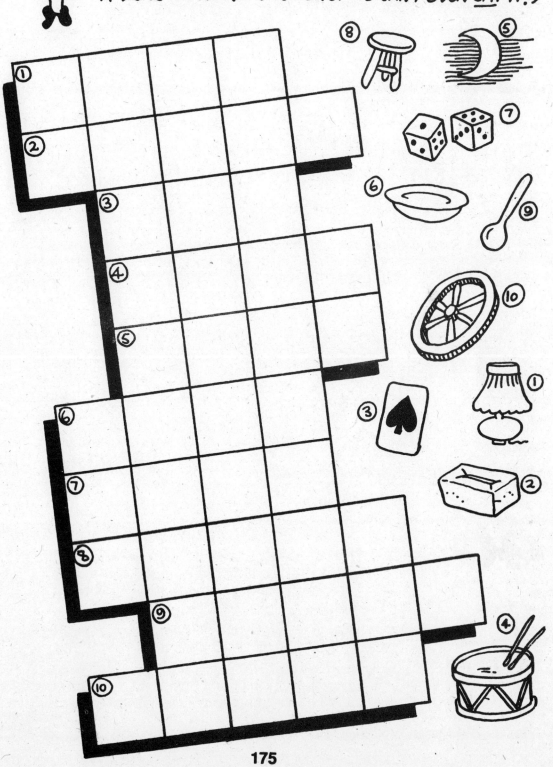

47

The Dead Sea is 47 miles (75.6 km) long and 10 miles (16 km) wide at its greatest breadth. The River Jordan flows into it, but the sea – the saltiest anywhere on Earth (few plants and no fish) – has no outlet.

A mosquito has forty-seven teeth.

The game of cricket has forty-seven rules.

Fit them in

FIT THE WORDS INTO THE CIRCLE.

HOW MANY KEYS?

How many keys has the locksmith dropped?

BREAKFAST JUMBLE

CAN YOU UNJUMBLE THESE ITEMS ON THE BREAKFAST TABLE?

MAJ
KILM
TUBERT
ESTROAT
GORPRIED
DRABE

PARTY GAMES

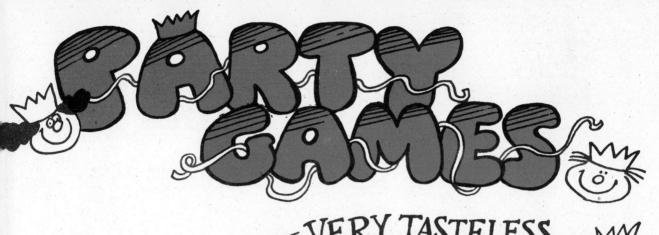

VERY TASTELESS

CUT UP CUBES OF CARROT, CHOCOLATE, APPLE, CHEESE, OR ANYTHING ELSE EDIBLE-LYING AROUND THE KITCHEN. ASK FOR A VOLUNTEER TO BE BLINDFOLDED AND ANOTHER TO HOLD THE VOLUNTEER'S NOSE.

WHEN HE CAN'T SEE OR SMELL, FEED HIM THE TITBITS AND GIVE HIM A POINT FOR EVERY ONE HE IDENTIFIES CORRECTLY.

PLAY UNTIL EVERYONE'S HAD A TURN. THE WINNER IS THE ONE WITH THE BEST PALATE.

ER.... FRIED OCTOPUS?

Swimming the Channel —by— Frances Near

KNOCK KNEES

Make two teams and give everyone a 2p piece. Line both teams up about 10 m (11 yds) from two buckets at the other side of the room or garden. On the word 'Go' the first player in each team puts the coin between his knees, runs to the bucket, drops the coin into it, and runs back. As soon as they return, the next players make their knock-kneed dash for the bucket. If a coin drops on the floor, whoever let it go has to start again.

Aches and Pains —by— Arthur Ritus

Superior Science

Science against destiny: who was the victor?

by W. Price

How do you get a ghost to lie perfectly flat? You use a spirit level.

The old horse put his head over a broken gate and watched the couple with his sad brown eyes. A boy and a girl, strolling hand in hand down a lane green with growing things, cool and hushed in the twilight. Hawthorn blossom creamed the hedgerows, filling the air with fragrance, a trill of belated birdsong trembled in the shadows; all nature awaited the coming of night.

Arms entwined, the couple paused by the gate, eyes filled with each other. The horse nuzzled them apart, demanding attention. Together they stroked his long, gentle face, accepting him into the magic of their moment.

A boy, a girl, and an old horse in a country lane. They never saw the great flash of light, brighter than a million suns, which split asunder the darkening sky and paralyzed every living thing on earth.

Every man, woman and child. The eagle in the clouds, the beetle beneath the stone; rainbow fish in sunlit seas, and shapeless creatures that crawled the dark floors of unfathomed deeps. Every tree, every flower, every blade of grass; all life on earth was frozen into immobility, suspended in a moment of time.

Ten thousand miles above the earth's surface a flying saucer sailed smoothly in orbit. Its commander turned to his lieutenant.

"Phase One complete?"

"All life on the planet completely immobilized," replied the lieutenant.

"Regrettable, but necessary," said the commander, switching off the paralyzing beam. "Merely a question of superior science."

Those were his last words before his entire spaceship was instantly vaporized into a cloud of random atoms.

Beyond the orbit of Pluto, on the fringe of the solar system, a giant spacecraft hung in the black abyss of deep space. Agra, Supreme Commander of Inter-Stellar Probe based on the dying satellite of the Pole Star, smiled his satisfaction.

"Someone else was interested in the third planet," he said. "Obviously a desirable site for intelligent life. Too bad they had to be destroyed, but our own need is imperative. Merely a question of superior science."

Agra issued orders to set the spacecraft on course for the earth, which it could reach in a matter of hours.

He felt confident this was the end of a long journey through space and time. For the first time in more than a thousand years members of his race would set foot outside the spacecraft. During that long period, generation after generation had lived and died in the tight, closed world of the spaceship, travelling at almost the speed of light across an immeasurable void. Their numbers were maintained at a

---

What is black, gushes out of the ground and shouts 'Excuse me'?
Refined oil.

Knock, knock.
Who's there?
Bella.
Bella who?
Bella not working, that's why I knocka.

What should you do with a blue monster?
Tell him a joke and cheer him up.

What do you get if an elephant sneezes?
Out of the way!

What did the hungry donkey say when it only had thistles to eat?
Thistle have to do.

What animal with two humps is found at the North Pole?
A lost camel.

Bert was dangling a fishing rod down a manhole. The vicar gave him 50p and asked with a smile, 'How many have you caught today?'
'You're the sixth,' said Bert.

What problem does a man who stands on his own two feet have?
He can't get his trousers on.

What did the dog say when it sat on the sandpaper?
Rough!

How do you make mice smell nice?
Use a mousewash.

What did you learn at school today? Alec's father asked him after his first day.
Not enough, Dad. I have to go back tomorrow.

constant level, evenly balanced between the sexes. Twenty-five men and twenty-five women, who had never felt the wind on their faces, enjoyed the scent of flowers or thrilled to a sunset. They knew all about these things, but only from the books and film records left by their remote ancestors who had first embarked on this epic voyage.

Agra and every member of his crew knew that their race had once lived on a green and pleasant planet, a world of flower-filled forests, where blue skies were alive with birdsong, and sparkling rivers flowed into foaming seas.

But the flowers faded in the forest, the skies grew silent, and vast sheets of ice spread over the seas. As their planet began to die, its inhabitants, who were a highly scientific people, sent out space probes in the hope that someday, somewhere in the universe, their race would find a new home on another planet. And this hope had been kept alive throughout the generations.

Once settled in a stable orbit round the earth, Agra examined the computer's analysis of surface conditions on the third planet. The rest of the crew stood in the main control room, waiting in respectful silence. They were all

alike, not more than five feet tall, with frail bodies which seemed hardly able to support their massive heads. They had little physical strength, but their brains were immensely powerful.

"Highly satisfactory," decided Agra. "The atmosphere has a high oxygen content, equal to that of our own planet at its best."

"But is it safe?" queried Spiro, his second-in-command. "The planet is populated. Is it not possible that we may be contaminated?"

Agra frowned. The thought had occurred to him. They

knew, of course that the sort of planet they needed would almost certainly already support higher forms of life. Contamination was a real danger. For many generations his people had been conditioned by the artificial, antiseptic atmosphere of the spacecraft.

"We shall not even need spacesuits or oxygen masks," he said. "But I see your point. I will land in some secluded spot, well away from large centres of population."

"I still think we will need protection," persisted Spiro.

Agra laughed. "Stop worrying, Spiro. Our superior mental powers will give us ample protection."

Spiro did not seem entirely convinced, but he held his tongue.

The computer indicated a suitable landing site in the northern hemisphere and the spacecraft put down safely in a wooded area nestling in a heap of hills.

Glancing at the computerized calendar, Agra made an entry in his log: "A landing on the third planet of star catalogue number Z233 successfully accomplished in the Polarian Year 8041."

Outside the spacecraft he breathed in deeply, the clean, country air swelling his lungs. The rest of the crew crowded out into the dawn of a fine summer day. For a while they stood in silent awe, drinking in the beauty of a reality which for so long had been only a dream. Then they went wild, rolling in the dew-wet grass, embracing trees, peering and probing into flowering hedgerows.

Agra called his crew to order and led them down a tree-lined lane flanked by neat green meadows where cows stood motionless.

"Very good of our late friends to immobilize all life for us," he chuckled. "Some primitive form of paralyzing ray, I suppose. Probably it will wear off shortly. Then we can begin our conquest of the planet."

They came across the young couple and the old horse by the broken gate.

"Ah — the aborigines," exclaimed Agra, walking up to the still forms of the boy and girl.

"Be careful!" warned Spiro.

Agra shrugged his shoulders. "They are very much like us, as might be expected under the physical conditions on this planet. Reasonably intelligent too, I suspect, but their brain capacity is limited."

He ran his hands over the boy's sturdy frame, realizing at once that in terms of physical strength this earthman was more than a match for any ten of his crew. He also knew that any one of his crew could reduce the earthman to a pile of ashes in a few seconds by sheer mental force.

"They are probably loaded with all sorts of germs," growled Spiro. "We should be wearing spacesuits."

Agra laughed. "Our superior science will triumph," he said.

Unprotected and unsuspecting, the aliens marched into the little hamlet of Eyam, in the Year of Our Lord 1665 — the year of the Great Plague . . .

48

The countdown for an American space flight begins forty-eight hours prior to launching. During this crucial period, the rocket is filled with fuel and all its numerous complicated parts are checked.

The definition of a hair's breadth is one forty-eighth part of an inch.

Lightning strikes the Empire State Building, New York, up to forty-eight times a year.

IT'S EASY...

HELP!!

... TO MAKE THE **STRONGEST** PERSON TOTALLY DEFENCELESS!!

STRONGO

All you have to do is get him to stand with his arms outstretched, palms downwards... now balance two full glasses of water on the backs of his hands....

GET OUT OF THAT, THEN!!

What did one eye say to the other?

Between you and me, something smells!

SNIFF... SNIFF...

did you hear about the man who bought a shock-proof, water-proof, unbreakable, anti-magnetic watch?

here, ticky, ticky!

He **lost** it!

NOUGHTS & CROSSES

Nine-square noughts and crosses grids soon become boring, especially if you always lose. Draw up a 36-square grid. You still have to complete a line of three noughts or crosses, horizontally, vertically or diagonally — but it's much more difficult.

All around

PIT THE PICTURE NAMES INTO THE EMPTY SQUARES.

49

The most memorable year of the Gold Rush in California was 1849. It is recalled in the once-popular song *Clementine*, and the miners of that year were known as 'forty-niners'.

The speed limit on Japanese motorways is only 49 mph (78.85 kph). Vehicles are driven on the left-hand side of the road.

Since 14 June 1818, the 49°N line of latitude – the famous 49th Parallel – has denoted the unguarded border between Canada and the USA.

MAKE A RAINBOW

The sun's light is made up of waves of seven different colours. Make your own rainbow and see what they are.

BALANCE A GLASS OF WATER ON A SUNNY WINDOW LEDGE WITH THE GLASS SLIGHTLY OVER THE INDOOR LEDGE.

PUT A LARGE SHEET OF PAPER ON THE FLOOR UNDER THE WINDOW. THE WATER ACTS AS A **PRISM**, BREAKING UP THE SUNBEAM INTO VIOLET, INDIGO, BLUE, GREEN, YELLOW, ORANGE AND RED.

JOIN THE DOTS

If you follow the dots from 1 to 61 with your pencil, you will find out who the Indian is mad at. If you want a bit more fun, just trace out the route first with your finger and see if you can guess what the answer is.

A British guardsman's bearskin, copied from those worn by French grenadiers at the Battle of Waterloo in 1815, is 50.8 cm (20 in) tall.

World swimming records can be set only in pools with a length of 50 m (164 ft).

As lions and gazelles can both reach a speed of 50 mph (80 kph), life and death for the latter becomes a question of stamina.

50

Answers

PAGE

5

WHOSE HAT?
A-6; B-3; C-5; D-1; E-4; F-2.

6
GIVE US A CLUE!
Number 10

7
BEE MAZE
r

9
PUT A SOCK IN IT!
1,6,10,13,17,20,22,23.

24
WRITING
Quill

25
SECRET CODE
Dallas

25
THEY ALL GO IN

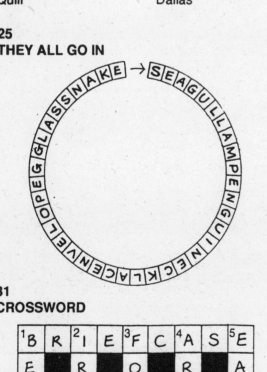

31
CROSSWORD

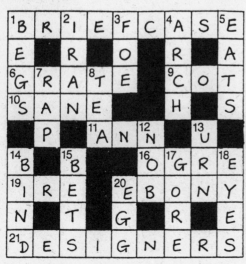

32
NOISES
Amplifier

36
IN THE DUCK POND
A and G

37
SNAIL COMES LAST
Octave

37
NINE LITTLE MEN
The sixth man is different; he has no ear.

41
FOLLOW THE BIRDS
Thrush, magpie, rook, crow, robin, skylark, swallow, swift, owl, goose, linnet, heron, jackdaw.

43
TRIPLETS
2, 4 and 5

44
FLOWER ARRANGEMENTS
Dandelion, buttercup, wallflower, pansy, hollyhock, tulip.

44
FINISH THE WORDS
1. Bud; 2. Leaf; 3. Onion; 4. Flower;
5. Pepper; 6. Squash; 7. Pumpkin.

46
PAINTERS
Gainsborough

47
ODD SHAPE
3 times

51
CHEF PUZZLE
Sugar, salt, pepper, mustard, salad dressing.

54
LEFT AND RIGHT
6 and 10; 3 and 18.

55
A PUZZLE FOR SID
Sid should have said 'wrong', not 'why'.

71
SPOT THE DIFFERENCES
1. Flash on boots.
2. Referee's hair.
3. Badge on referee's shirt.
4. Shirt on fallen player.
5. Floodlights on stand.
6. Writing on notebook.

71
HOW?
One of them must get up and go and lie beside the other - so the bone is then on the outside.

71
FIVE BECOMES FOUR

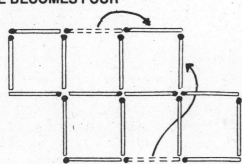

72
MARATHON MATT!
29 doughnuts

73
CIRCULAR
Crab, balloon, nest, tortoise, elephant, toucan, nurse, egg.

73
REFLECTIONS

75
FLOWERS
1. Daisy; 2. Tulip; 3. Aster; 4. Lupin; 5. Pansy.

75
IN A QUANDARY
Mr White's dog is black - Mr Black's dog is white.

79
FOUR PATTERNS
Number 2

79
THINK OF A NUMBER

| | | + | = 12

82
KEEPING TOGETHER
Pins

82
MATCH THE SHADOW
Number 5

84
BALLOONS
Number 2

84
A SPOTTY PUZZLE
Rows B and G are the same.

84
RHYMING PAIRS
Snail, pail; sock, lock; hook, book; bun, gun.

87
HOW MANY BRICKS?
92

88
ALL JUMBLED UP
1 and 4 will not tangle. 2 and 3 will tangle.

96
GO BY WATER
Rowing

112
SOUP
Tomato

113
ODD ONE OUT
Fish, peas, fork.

113
COUNTRY FOOD
A4, B1, C5, D2, E3.

114
GIRLS NAMES
Jane, Mary, Rita.

114
THE EXPLORER
'Watch out for the dinosaurs!'

114
NAME THE COUNTRIES
Denmark, Ireland, Canada, Wales.

114
FIND THE BIRD!
Lark, swan, cuckoo, magpie, kestrel, robin, barn owl.

116
SPOT THE DIFFERENCES
1. Television lens.
2. Lettering on television.
3. Bow tie.
4. Number on card.
5. Star.

116
WHAT IS HIDDEN HERE?
A baker.

116
MYSTERY MEN
Number 5

118
FINISH THE SAYINGS
Owl, rake, bell, fiddle, eel.

118
SIX DIFFERENCES
1. One butterfly has dots.
2. A skier appears on Mount Fuji.
3. Two leaves instead of three.
4. Umbrella handle longer.
5. Child appears on bridge.
6. Dress pattern has changed.

119
PLACE THE WORDS

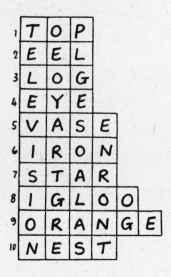

119
COIN PUZZLE
Move coins 1 and 4 down beside numbers 8 and 9. Then place number 10 over the top of numbers 2 and 3. Now the triangle is pointing in the opposite direction.

120
OUT OF ORDER
Pell Mell

124
A SHIP'S LANTERNS
Green

125
NURSERY RHYME CROSSWORD
Across: 1. Buns, 2. Dumpty, 6. Bo Peep, 7. Tom, 9. Nut, 10. Owl.
Down: 1. Boy Blue, 2. Humpty, 3. Bye, 5. Spoon, 8. Moon.

126
ANIMAL WORLD
1. Skunk, 2. Beaver, 3. Mole, 4. Weasel, 5. Otter, 6. Ferret, 7. Mink.

130
SPOT THE ODD ONE OUT
The hammer - all other items are used in the kitchen.

130
ZOO SIGNS
Giraffe, crocodile, monkey, elephant, zebra, lion, camel.

132
ABOUT BOATS
Skipper

135
LAZY ANGLER
A-fish; B-boot; C-eel.

135
WHAT DO YOU SEE?
Two profiles.

135
THE PALETTE
1. Brown, 2. Yellow, 3. Purple, 4. Green, 5. Crimson, 6. Magenta, 7. Indigo, 8. Violet.

139
MATCH THE SHADOW
Number 3